At Sylvan, we believe that a lifelong love of learning begins at an early age, and we are glad you have chosen our resources to help your children experience both the joy of mathematics and the joy of reading as they build these critical skills. We know that the time you spend with your children reinforcing the lessons learned in school will contribute to their love of learning.

A love of learning will translate into academic achievement. Successful readers are ready for the world around them; they are prepared to do research, to experience literature, and to make the connections necessary to achieve in school and life. Similarly, success in math requires more than just memorizing basic facts and algorithms; it also requires children to make sense of sizes, shapes, and numbers as they appear in the world. Children who can connect their understanding of math to the world around them will be ready for the challenges of mathematics as they advance to more complex topics.

At Sylvan we use a research-based, step-by-step process in teaching that includes thought-provoking reading selections, math problems, and activities. As students increase their success as learners, they become more confident. With increasing confidence, students build even more success. The design of the Sylvan workbooks will help you to help your children build the skills and confidence that will contribute to success in school.

We're excited to partner with you to support the development of confident, well-prepared, independent learners!

The Sylvan Team

Sylvan Learning Center

Build the skills, habits, and attitudes your child needs to succeed in school and in life.

Sylvan Learning is the leading provider of tutoring and supplemental education services to students of all ages and skill levels. At Sylvan, our warm and caring tutors tailor individualized learning plans that build the skills, habits, and attitudes students need to succeed in school and in life. Affordable tutoring instruction is available in math, reading, writing, study skills, homework help, test prep, and more at more than 900 learning centers in the United States, Canada, and abroad.

The proven, personalized approach of our in-center programs delivers unparalleled results that other supplemental education services simply can't match. Your child's achievements will be seen not only in test scores and report cards but outside the classroom as well. You will see a new level of confidence in all of your child's activities and interactions.

At Sylvan, we want your child to be successful at every stage of his or her academic journey. Here's a glimpse into how our program works:

- Depending on your needs and your child's needs, we'll do an assessment to pinpoint skill gaps, strengths, and focus areas.

- We develop a customized learning plan designed to meet your child's academic goals.

- Through our method of skill mastery, your child will not only learn and master the skills in the personalized plan but he or she will be truly motivated and inspired to achieve.

- Our teachers are caring and highly qualified. We'll get to know your child and keep lessons fresh and fun.

- Every step of the way, we'll work together to evaluate your child's progress and learning goals.

To learn more about Sylvan and our innovative in-center programs, call 1-800-EDUCATE or visit www.SylvanLearning.com. **With over 900 locations in North America, there is a Sylvan Learning Center near you!**

Kindergarten
Numbers & Sight Words
Workout

Published in the United States by Penguin Random House LLC and
in Canada by Penguin Random House Canada Limited, Toronto.

Kindergarten Numbers & Counting and *Kindergarten Sucess with Sight Words*
were first published separately by Sylvan, in 2011 and 2012.

Created by Smarterville Productions LLC

Random House and the colophon are registered trademarks of Penguin Random House LLC

Producer: TJ Trochlil McGreevy

Producer & Editorial Direction: The Linguistic Edge

Writers: Amy Craft and Christina Wilsdon

Cover and Interior Illustrations: Tim Goldman, Shawn Finley, and Duendes del Sur

Layout and Art Direction: SunDried Penguin

First Edition

ISBN: 978-1-5247-5855-4

www.sylvanlearning.com

This book is available at special discounts for bulk purchases for sales promotions or premiums.
For more information, write to Special Markets/Premium Sales, 1745 Broadway, MD 6-2,
New York, New York 10019 or e-mail specialmarkets@randomhouse.com.

MANUFACTURED IN CHINA

10 9 8 7 6 5 4 3 2

Kindergarten
Numbers & Counting

Contents

Numbers 1 to 10

Hello to Number 1

There is one horse in the picture. DRAW one horn to change the horse to a unicorn. Then WRITE the number 1 next to your drawing.

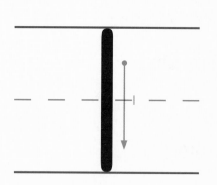

Hello to Number 2

There are two fishbowls in the picture. DRAW two fish so that there is one fish swimming in each bowl. Then WRITE the number **2** next to your drawing.

Hello to Number 3

There are three flowerpots in the picture. DRAW three flowers so that there is one flower in each pot. Then WRITE the number **3** next to your drawing.

Hello to Number 4

There are four bowls in the picture. DRAW four scoops of ice cream so that there is one scoop in each bowl. Then WRITE the number 4 next to your drawing.

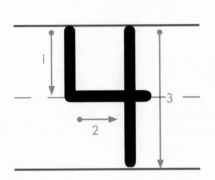

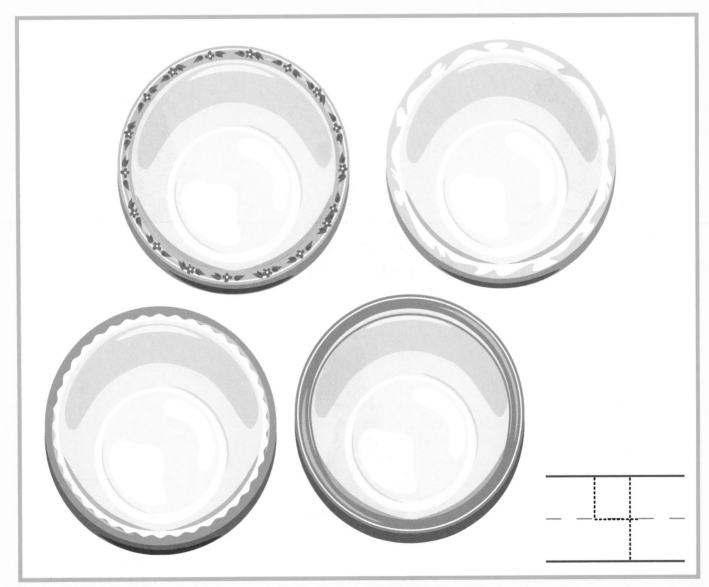

Numbers 1 to 10

Hello to Number 5

There are five dogs in the picture. DRAW five bones next to the dogs so that each dog gets one bone. Then WRITE the number **5** next to your drawing.

Hello to Number 6

There are six clowns in the picture. DRAW six balloons so that each clown is holding one balloon. Then WRITE the number **6** next to your drawing.

Hello to Number 7

There are seven skateboards in the picture. DRAW seven lightning bolts so that there is one lightning bolt on each skateboard. Then WRITE the number **7** next to your drawing.

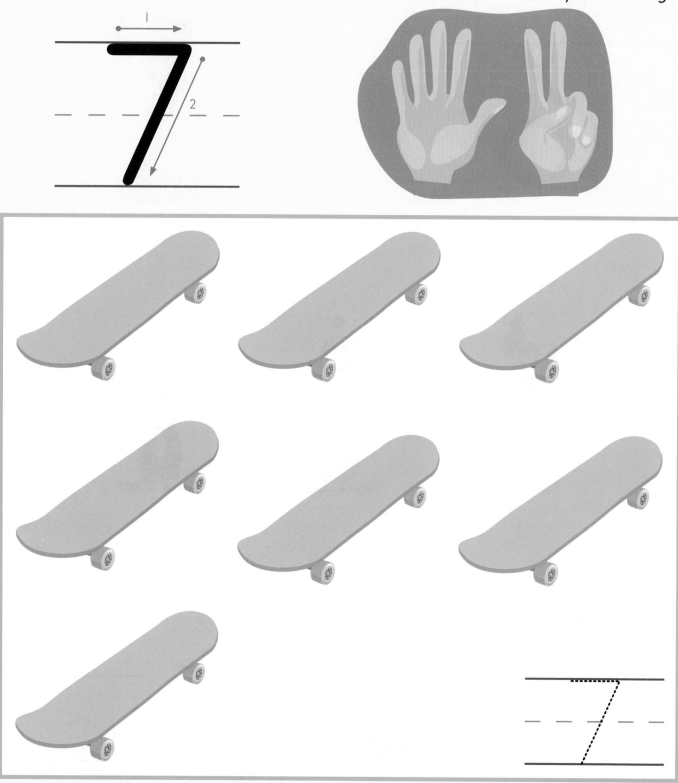

Hello to Number 8

There are eight bunnies in the picture. DRAW eight carrots next to the bunnies so that each bunny gets one carrot. Then WRITE the number **8** next to your drawing.

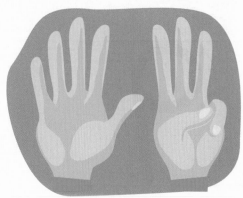

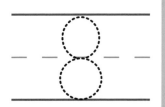

Hello to Number 9

There are nine plates in the picture. DRAW nine apples so that there is one apple on each plate. Then WRITE the number **9** next to your drawing.

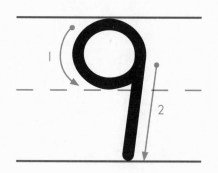

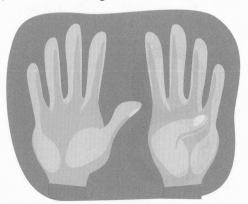

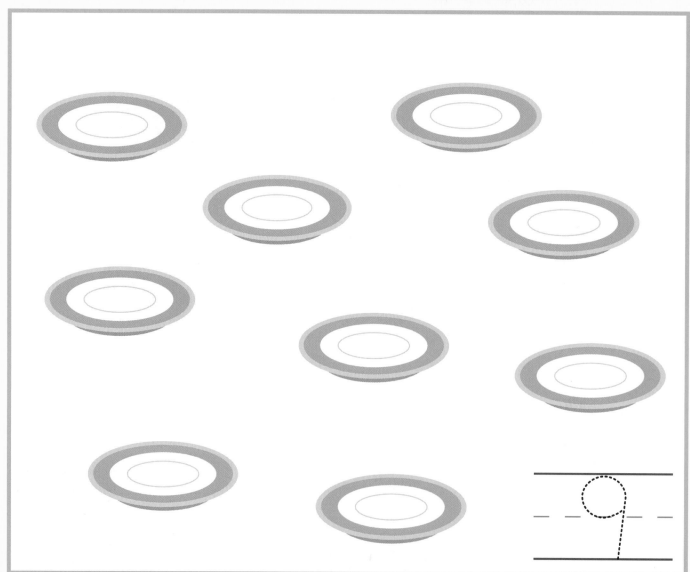

Hello to Number 10

There are ten cars in the picture. DRAW ten stars so that there is one star on each car. Then WRITE the number **10** next to your drawing.

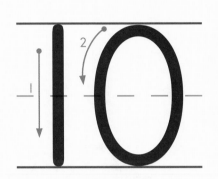

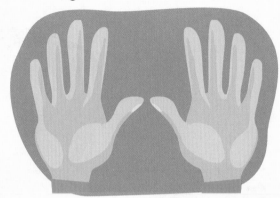

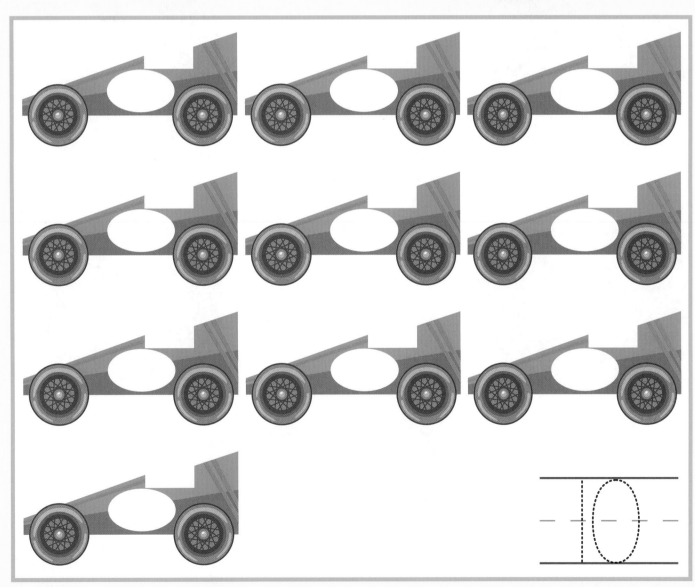

Nice Nests

COUNT the eggs in each nest. DRAW a line from the number **1** to each nest that has exactly one egg.

Stripey Socks

COUNT the blue stripes on each sock. CIRCLE all of the socks that have exactly two blue stripes.

Spot the Bugs

COUNT the spots on each bug. CIRCLE all of the bugs that have exactly three spots.

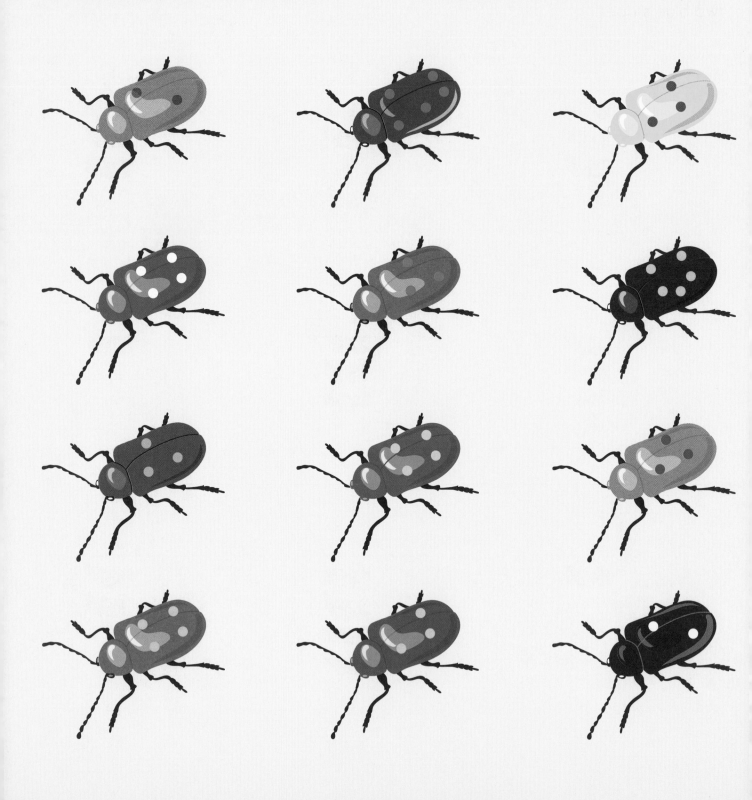

So Many Marbles

COUNT the marbles in each jar. DRAW a line from the number **4** to each jar that has exactly four marbles.

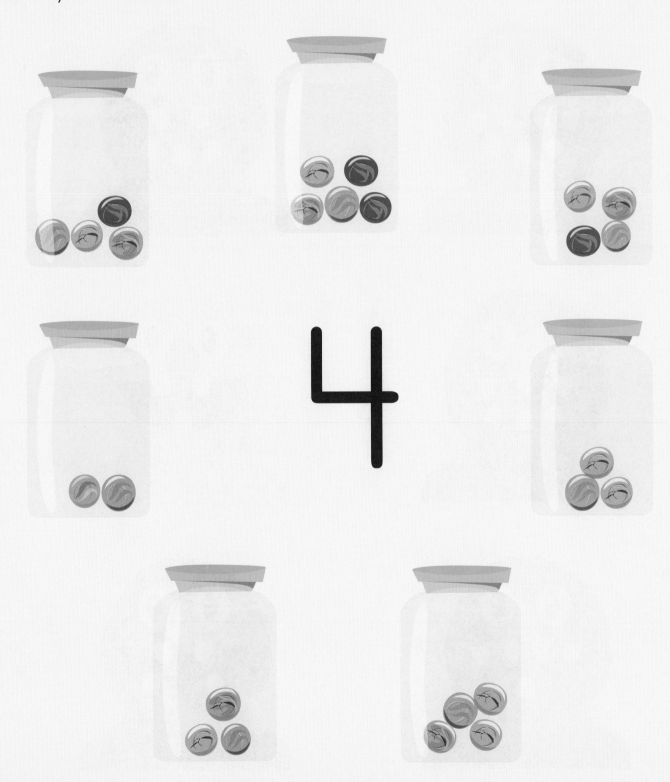

Monster Mouths

COUNT the teeth in each monster's mouth. CIRCLE all of the monsters that have exactly five teeth.

2

Special Delivery

COUNT the objects on the side of each truck. DRAW a line to connect each box with the truck where it belongs.

Delicious Doughnuts

COUNT the doughnuts in each box. DRAW a line from the number **6** to each box that has exactly six doughnuts.

Strawberry Snack

COUNT the strawberries in each bowl. CIRCLE all of the bowls that have exactly seven strawberries.

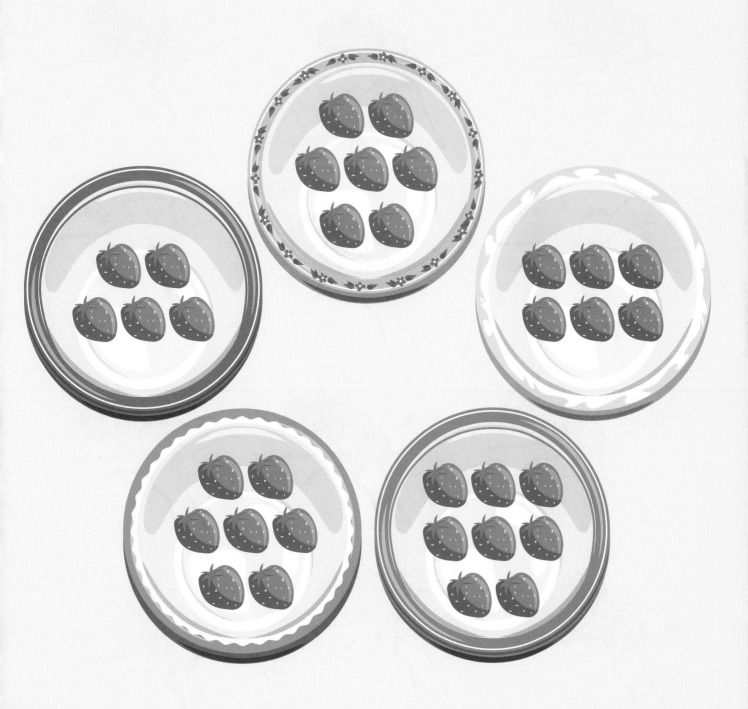

Spot the Bugs

COUNT the spots on each bug. CIRCLE all of the bugs that have exactly eight spots.

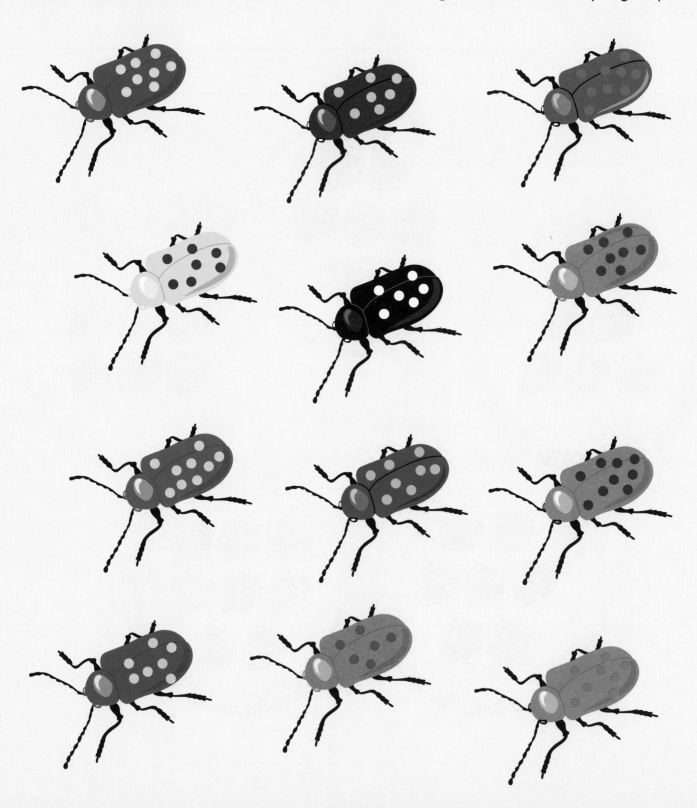

So Many Marbles

COUNT the marbles in each jar. DRAW a line from the number **9** to each jar that has exactly nine marbles.

Pretty as a Peacock

COUNT the feathers on each peacock's tail. CIRCLE all of the peacocks that have exactly 10 tail feathers.

Special Delivery

COUNT the objects on the side of each truck. DRAW a line to connect each box with the truck where it belongs.

Hello to Zero

DRAW a toy box that has zero toys in it. Then WRITE the number **0** next to your drawing.

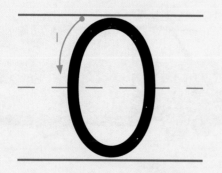

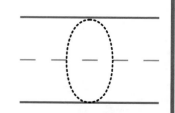

Today's Catch

CIRCLE all of the pictures that show **zero**.

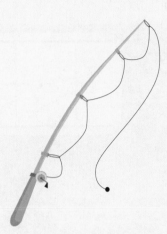

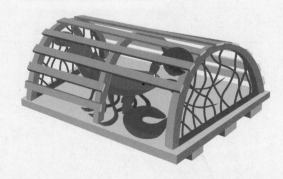

Ordinal Numbers

Along the Track

An ordinal number shows order or position, as in "*first* stop." TRACE the ordinal number that goes with each train station along the train track.

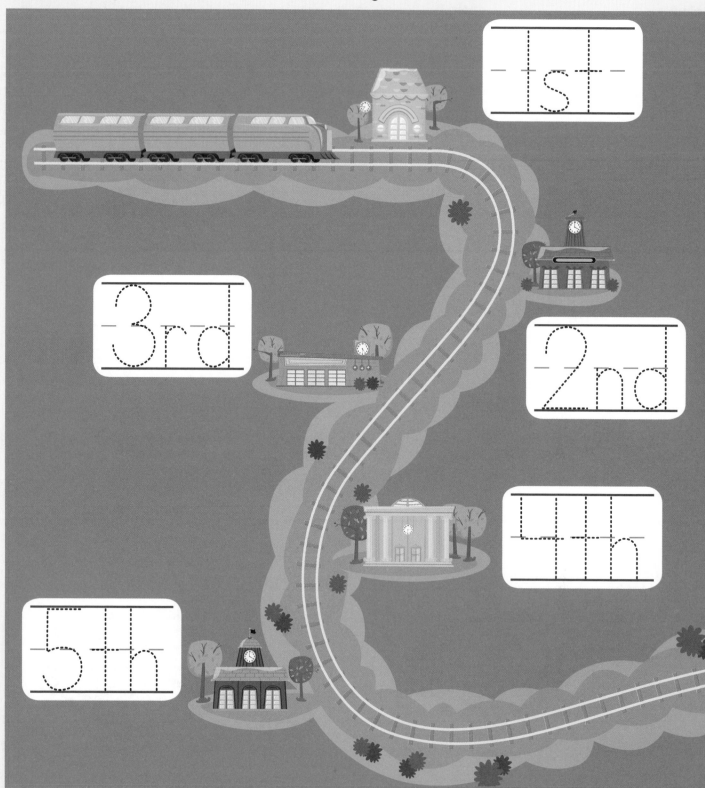

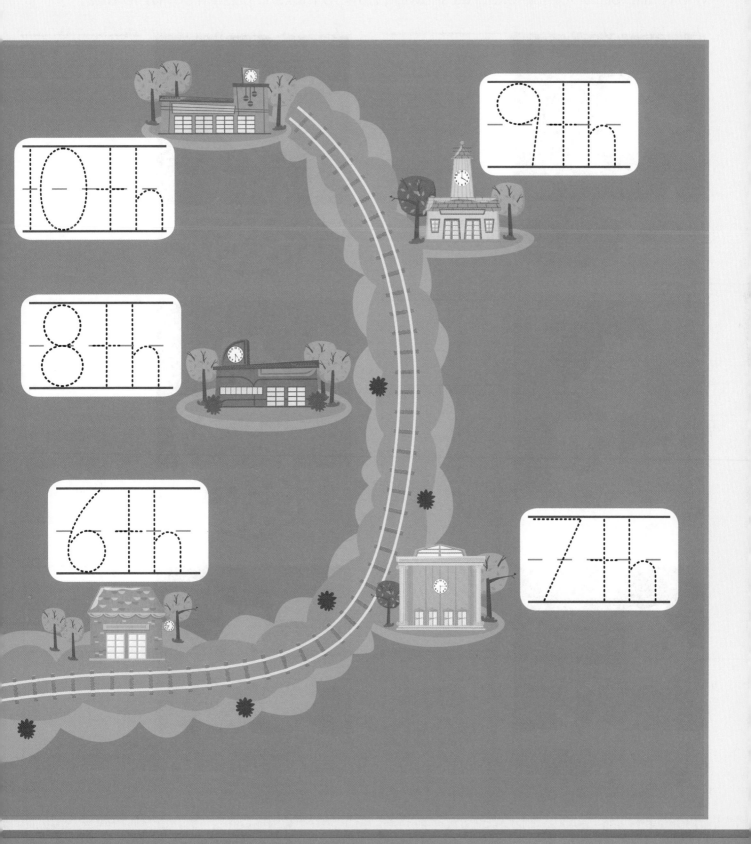

Pizza Party

WRITE the order of the pictures showing how to make a pizza from **1st** to **6th**.

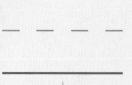

1

2

3

4

5

6

Sled Hill

LOOK at the picture at the top. Then WRITE the ordinal number for each person's place in line.

   4th

1

   _____

2

   _____

3

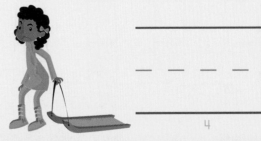   _____

4

Paint the Fence

COLOR each fence post according to the directions.

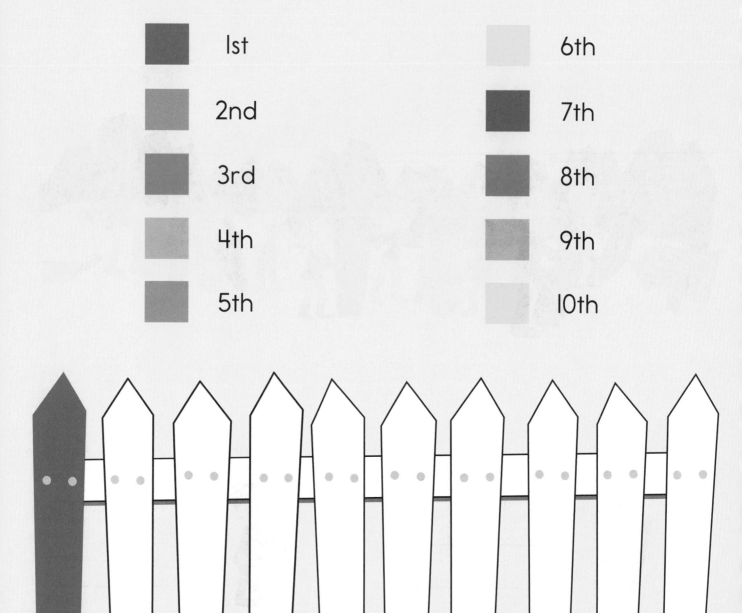

Race Runners

LOOK at the picture at the top. Then CIRCLE the runner that matches each ordinal number.

1. 1st

2. 5th

3. 10th

4. 3rd

5. 9th

6. 7th

Monster Mouths

DRAW a line to connect each number with a monster that has the same number of teeth.

1

2

3

4

5

Spot the Bugs

LOOK at the number in each row. CIRCLE the bug that has the same number of spots.

1

2

3

4

5

Pretty as a Peacock

DRAW a line to connect each number with a peacock that has the same number of tail feathers.

6

7

8

9

10

So Many Marbles

LOOK at the number in each row. CIRCLE the jar that has the same number of marbles.

6

7

8

9

10

Disappearing Rabbits

DRAW a line between the **0** and each hat that has zero rabbits.

Beautiful Balloons

COLOR each balloon according to the directions.

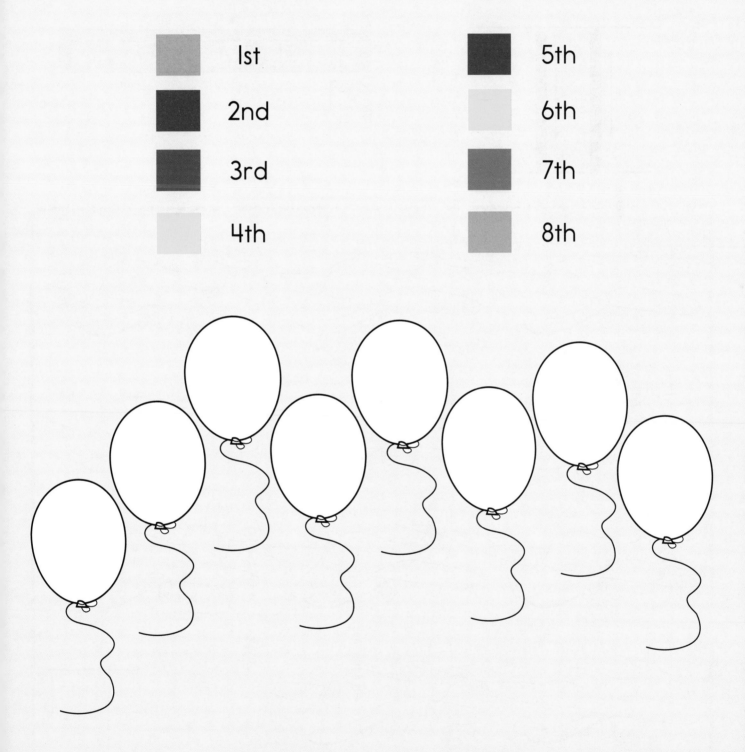

1st   5th

2nd   6th

3rd   7th

4th   8th

Numbers 11 to 20

Hello to Number 11

There are 11 airplanes in the picture. COLOR the airplanes 11 different colors. Then WRITE the number 11 next to your picture.

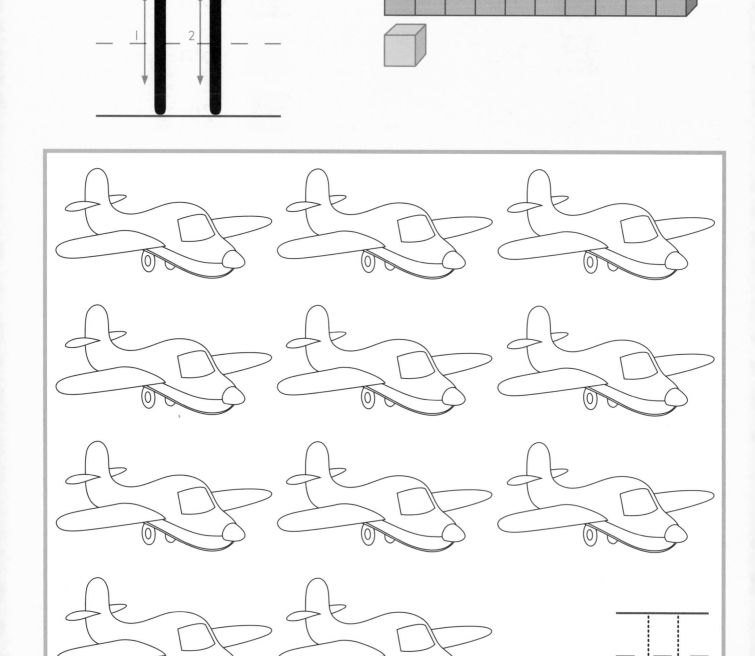

Hello to Number 12

There are 12 eggs in the picture. COLOR the eggs 12 different colors. Then WRITE the number 12 next to your picture.

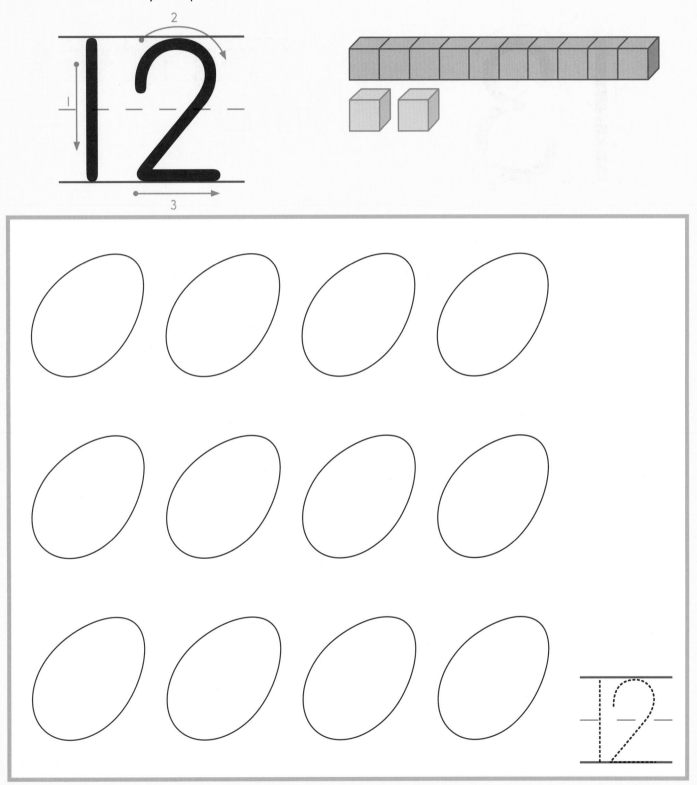

Hello to Number 13

There are 13 worms in the picture. COLOR the worms 13 different colors. Then WRITE the number **13** next to your picture.

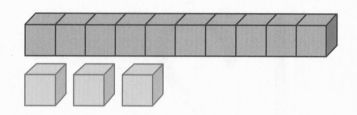

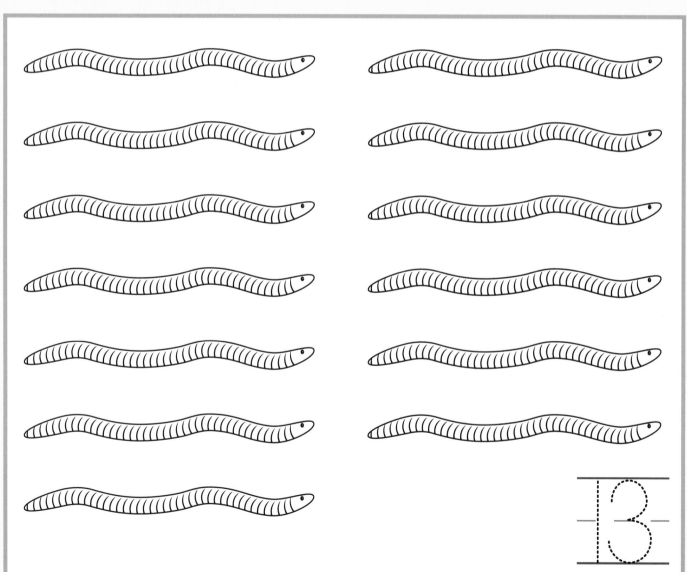

Hello to Number 14

There are 14 cars in the picture. COLOR the cars 14 different colors. Then WRITE the number 14 next to your picture.

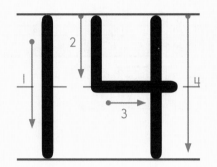

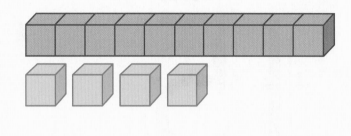

Hello to Number 15

There are 15 butterflies in the picture. COLOR the butterflies 15 different colors. Then WRITE the number **15** next to your picture.

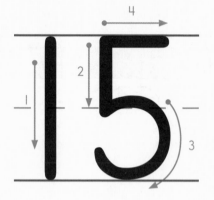

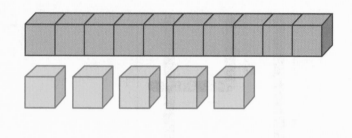

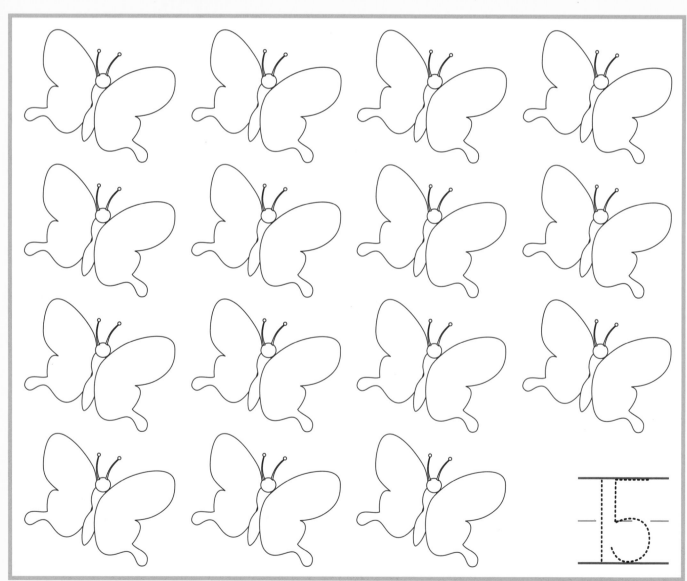

Hello to Number 16

There are 16 mittens in the picture. COLOR the mittens 16 different colors. Then WRITE the number **16** next to your picture.

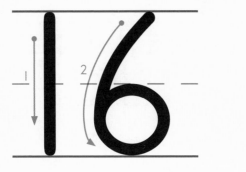

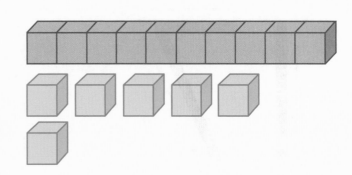

Hello to Number 17

There are 17 balloons in the picture. COLOR the balloons 17 different colors. Then WRITE the number 17 next to your picture.

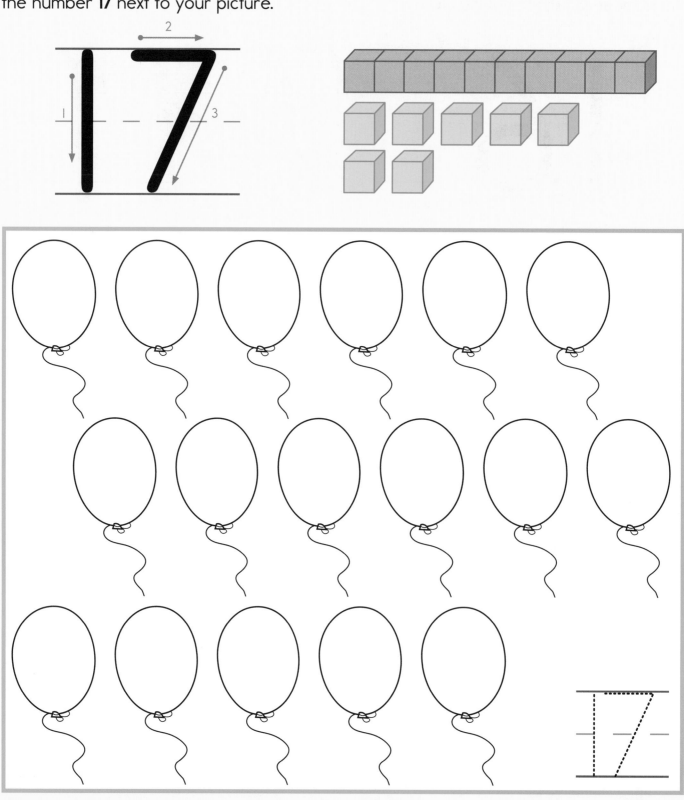

5

Hello to Number 18

There are 18 beetles in the picture. COLOR the beetles 18 different colors. Then WRITE the number **18** next to your picture.

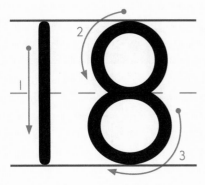

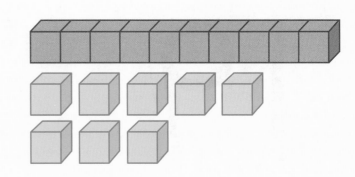

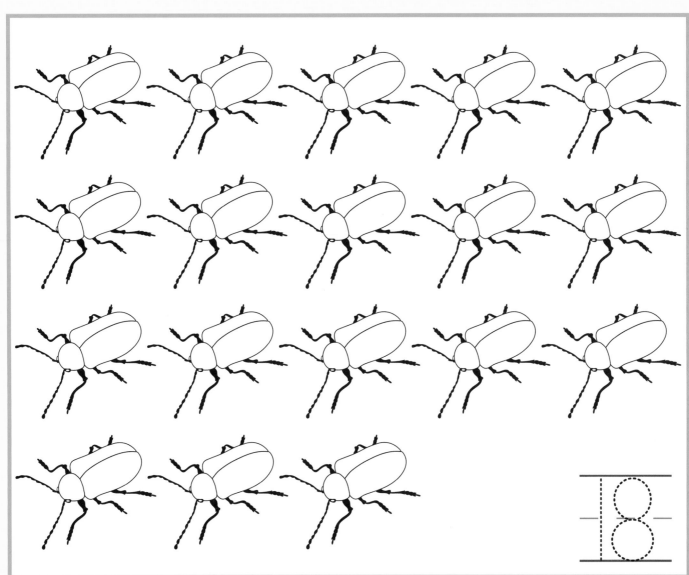

Hello to Number 19

There are 19 yo-yos in the picture. COLOR the yo-yos 19 different colors. Then WRITE the number **19** next to your picture.

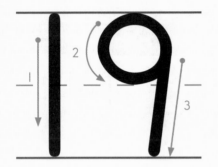

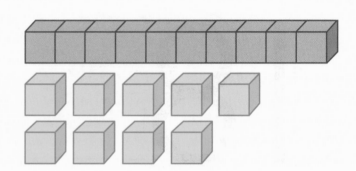

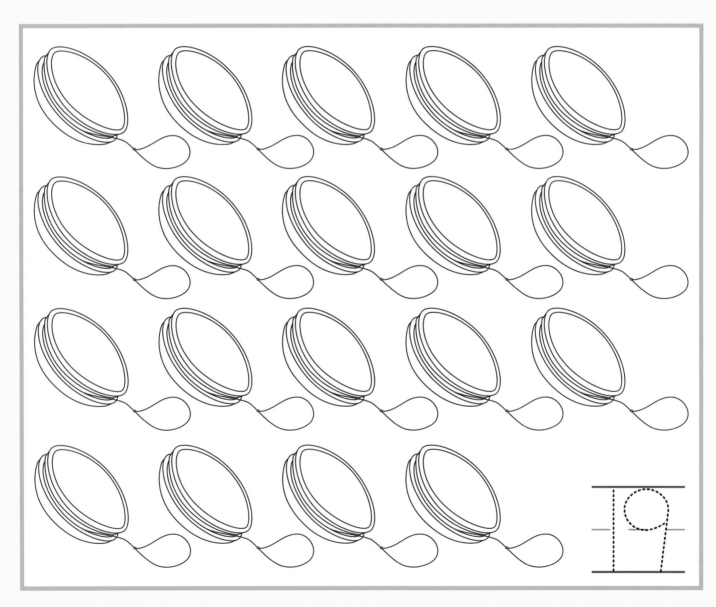

5

Hello to Number 20

There are 20 jellybeans in the picture. COLOR the jellybeans 20 different colors. Then WRITE the number **20** next to your picture.

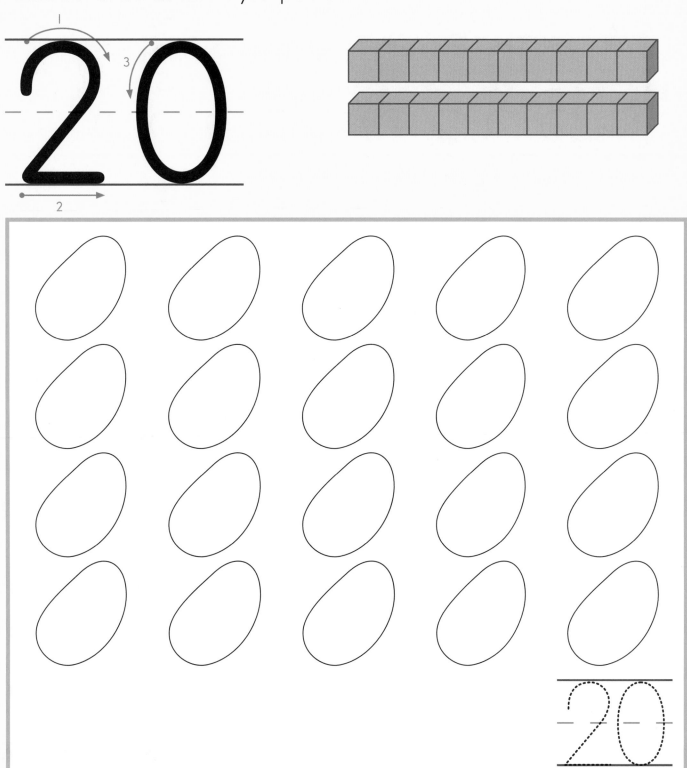

Ball Bonanza

LOOK at each number. CIRCLE the correct number of pictures to match the number.

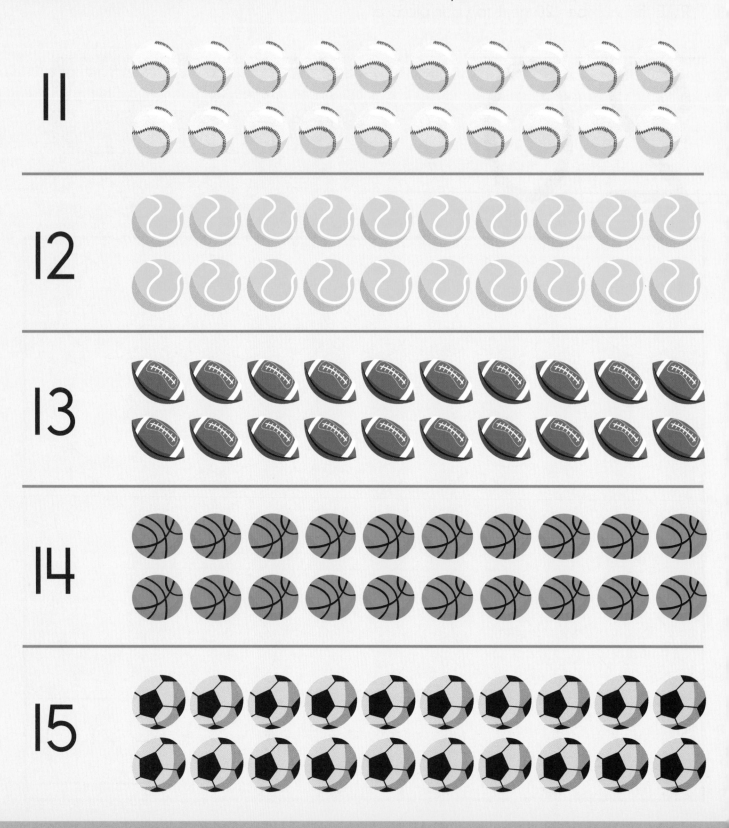

11

12

13

14

15

6

Bug Swarm

COUNT the number of each kind of bug. WRITE the number under each bug.

1

2

3

Flower Power

COUNT the number of petals on each flower, and WRITE the number below each flower. Then COLOR the flowers.

6

More than Enough

There are too many treats with each number. LOOK at the number. Then CROSS OUT the extra treats.

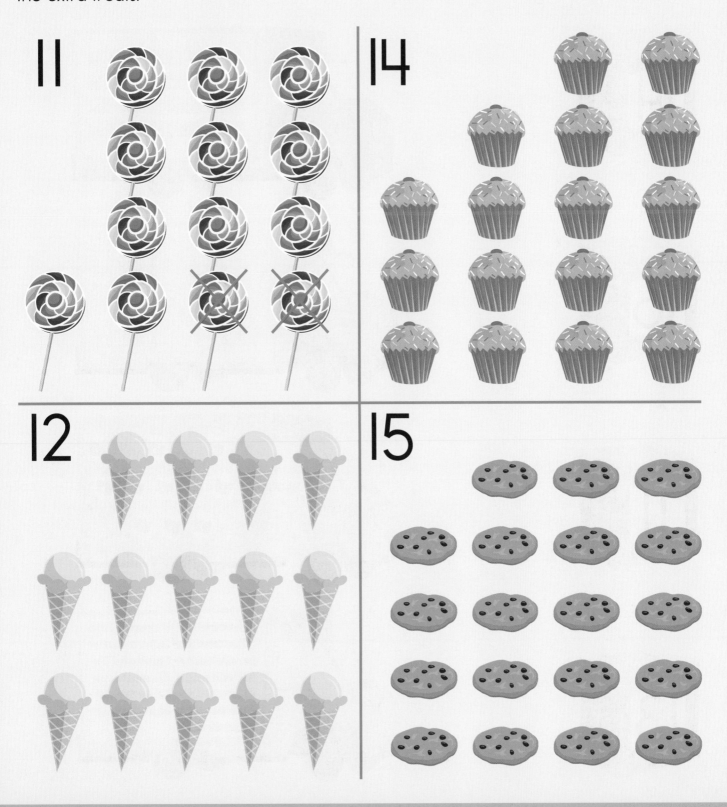

Special Delivery

COUNT the objects on the side of each truck. DRAW a line to connect each box with the truck where it belongs.

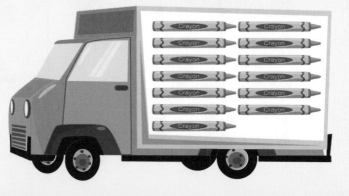

Button Up

LOOK at each number. CIRCLE the correct number of pictures to match the number.

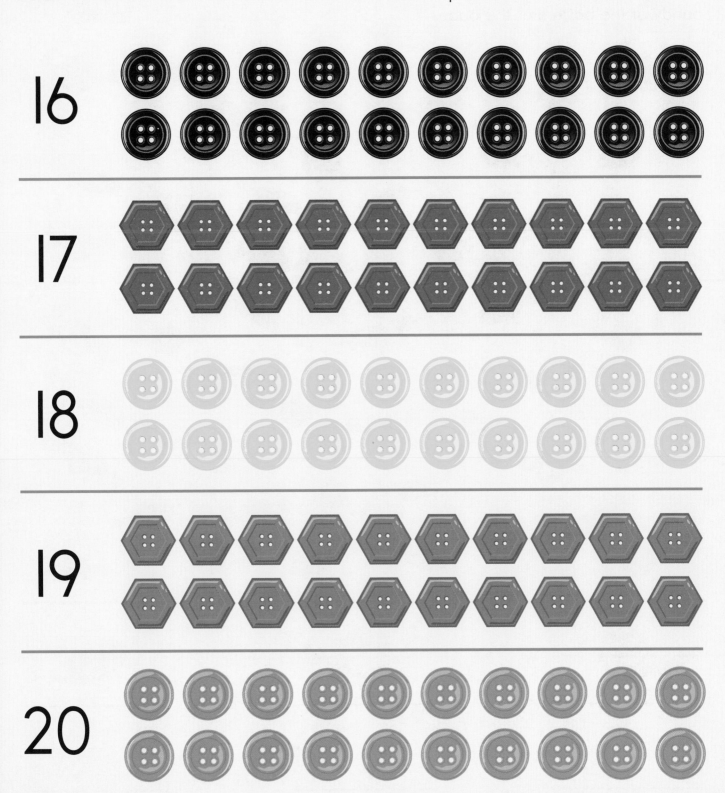

16

17

18

19

20

Candy Count

COUNT the number of each color of candy. WRITE the total number of each color of candy at the bottom of the page.

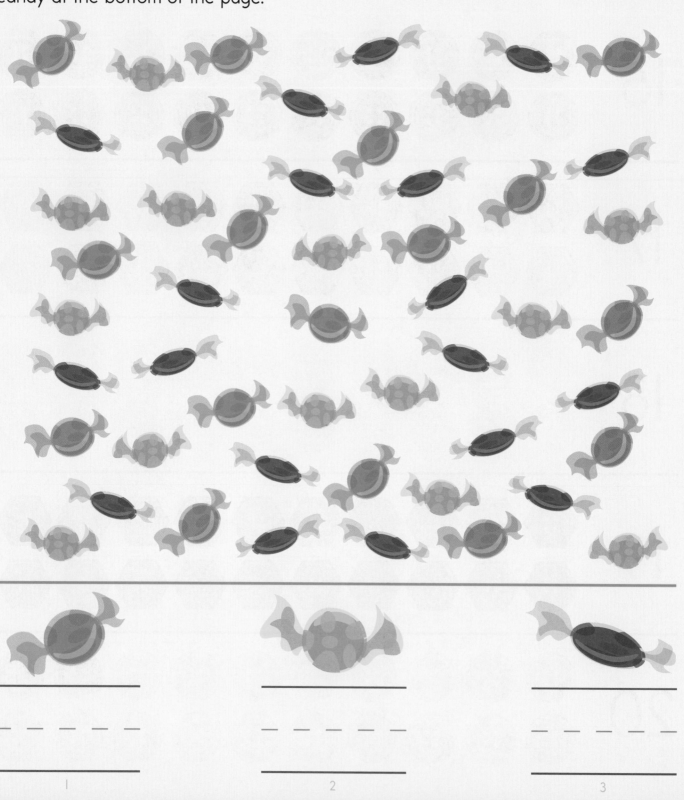

1 _____

2 _____

3 _____

6

Flower Power

COUNT the number of petals on each flower, and WRITE the number below each flower. Then COLOR the flowers.

1

2

3

4

More than Enough

There are too many toys with each number. LOOK at the number. Then CROSS OUT the extra toys.

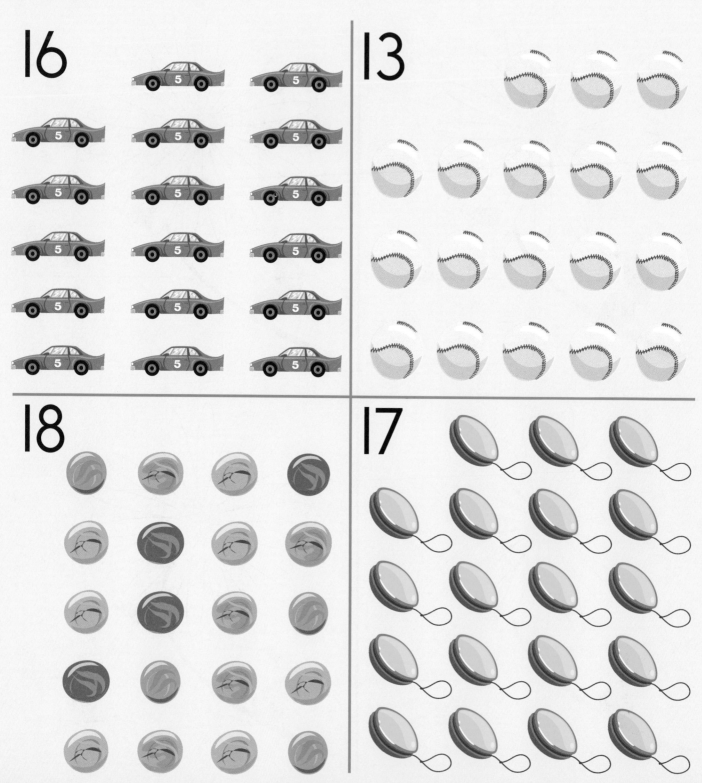

Special Delivery

COUNT the objects on the side of each truck. DRAW a line to connect each box with the truck where it belongs.

Seeing Stars

LOOK at each number. COLOR the correct number of stars to match the number.

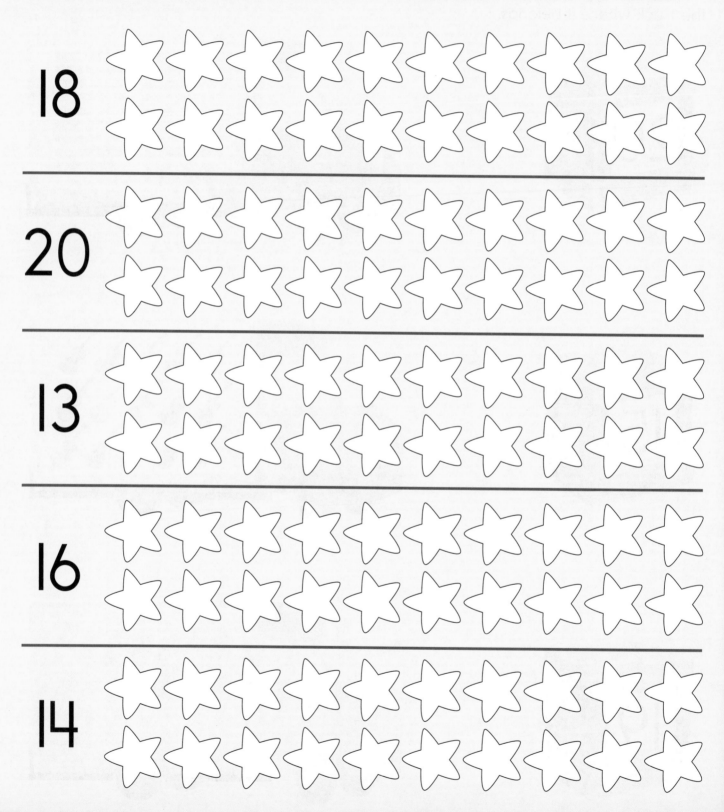

18

20

13

16

14

11

17

12

19

15

Bug Swarm

COUNT the number of each kind of bug. WRITE the total number of each type of bug at the bottom of the page.

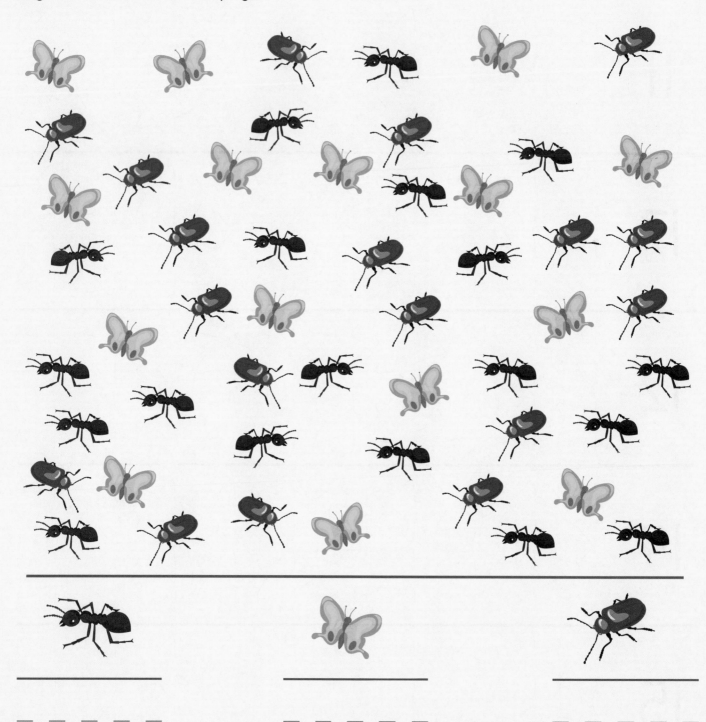

1 _____

2 _____

3 _____

Fruit Fun

LOOK at each number. CIRCLE the correct number of pictures to match the number.

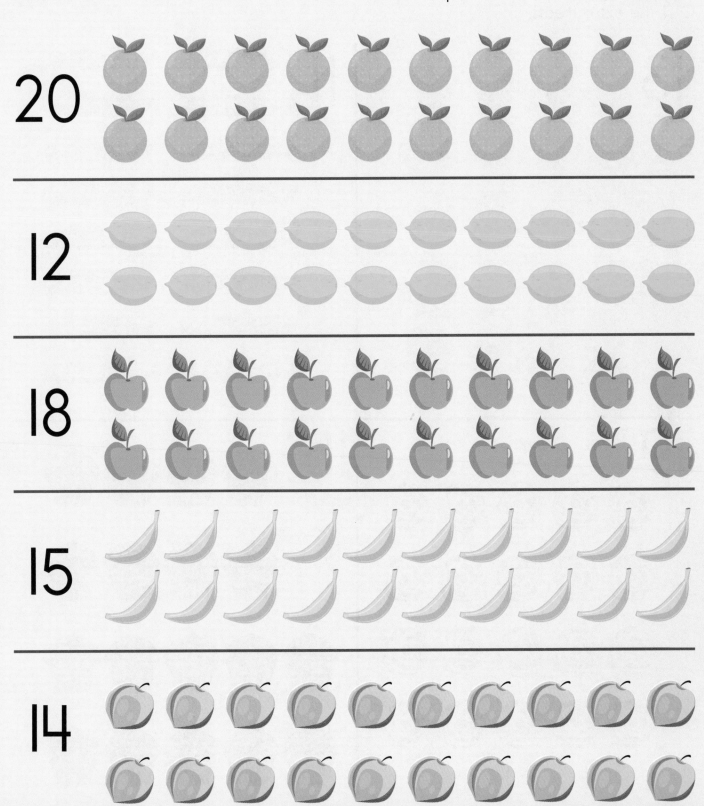

20

12

18

15

14

More than Enough

There are too many treats with each number. LOOK at the number. Then CROSS OUT the extra treats.

13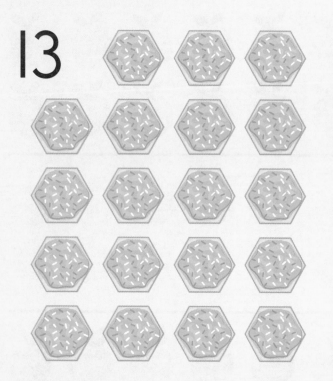

11

19

15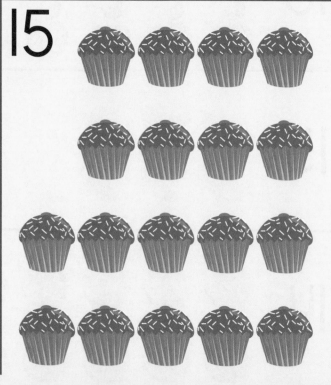

Special Delivery

COUNT the objects on the side of each truck. DRAW a line to connect each box with the truck where it belongs.

Number Patterns

Cargo Train

WRITE the missing numbers to complete each pattern.

Number Paths

WRITE the missing numbers to complete each pattern.

1 2 3 4 5 __

__ 4 5 6 7 8

5 6 __ 8 9 10

2 __ 4 5 6 7

4 5 6 7 __ 9

Number Patterns

Shelf Switcheroo

There's one book out of place in each row. CIRCLE the book with the wrong number.

1. 2   3   4   8   6   7

2. 5   6   7   8   6   10

3. 7   9   10   11   12   13

4. 10   9   8   9   6   5

5. 7   6   5   4   3   1

Number Paths

WRITE the missing numbers to complete each pattern.

Path 1: 1, 2, ___, 4, 5, ___, 7, 8, 9

Path 2: 5, ___, 7, 8, ___, 10, 11, ___, 13

Path 3: 7, 8, 9, ___, 11, 12, ___, 14, ___

Path 4: ___, 12, 13, 14, ___, 16, 17, ___, 19

Number Patterns

What Floor, Please?

WRITE the missing numbers next to the elevator buttons.

Number Paths

WRITE the missing numbers to complete the pattern.

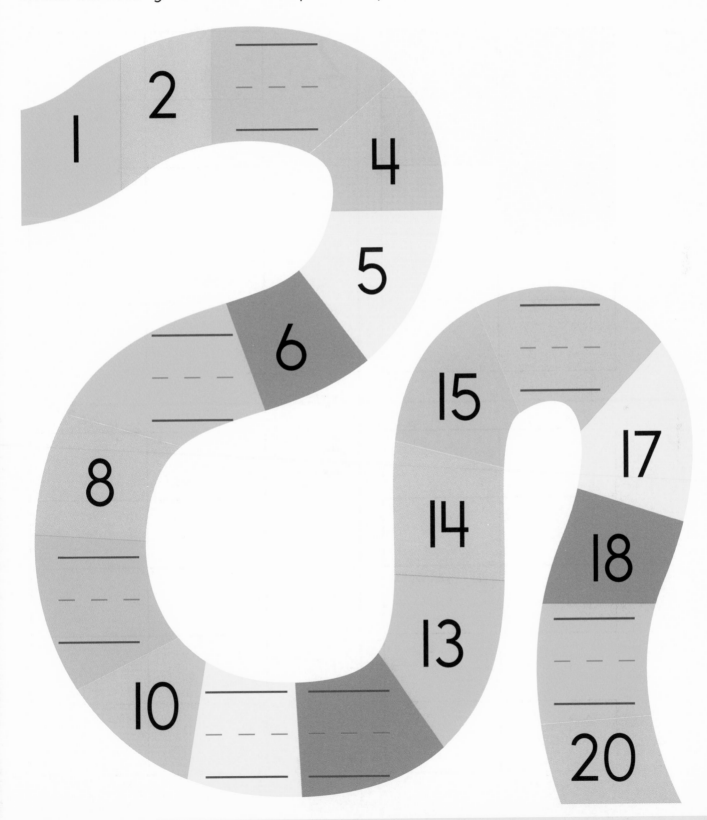

Color the Numbers

COLOR the boxes to match each number. Color across each row, starting with the top row.

5

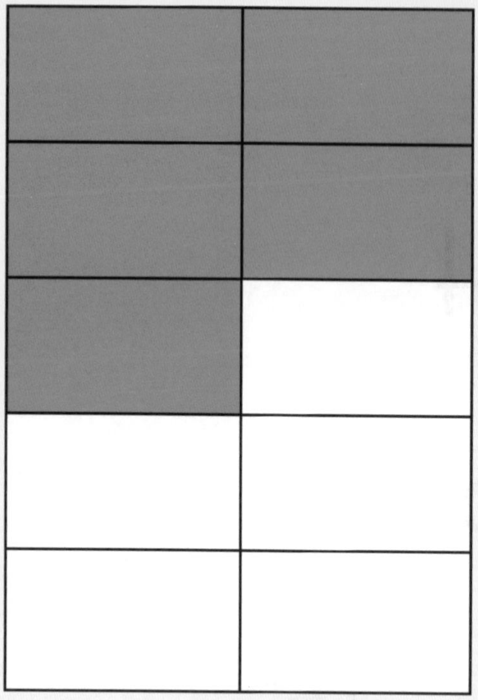

2

7

6

3

8

4

9

Two Can Share

An even number of items can be shared equally by two people. An odd number of items cannot be shared equally by two people. There will always be one extra item. CIRCLE **even** or **odd** for each group.

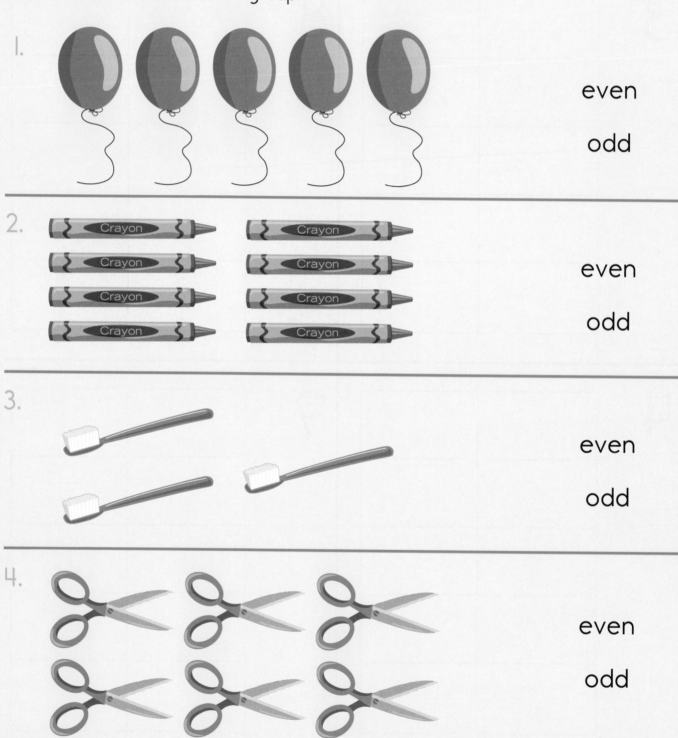

1. even

odd

2. even

odd

3. even

odd

4. even

odd

Odd Aliens

CIRCLE the aliens that have an odd number of arms.

Honey Hives

CIRCLE each beehive that has an even number of bees flying outside of it.

Number Paths

WRITE the missing numbers to complete each pattern.

First WRITE the missing odd numbers.

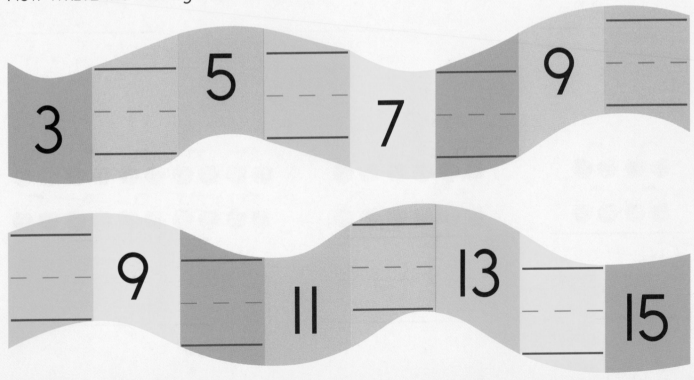

Now WRITE the missing even numbers.

Counting by Twos

Very Cherry

Counting is faster if you count by twos.

$$2 \quad 4 \quad 6 \quad 8 \quad 10 \quad 12 \quad 14 \quad 16 \quad 18 \quad 20$$

There are 20 cherries.

COUNT the cherries by twos. Then WRITE the number.

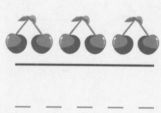

_____

- - - - - - - - -

_____

1

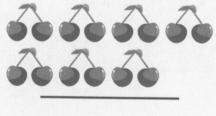
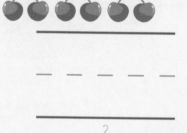

_____

- - - - - - - - -

_____

2

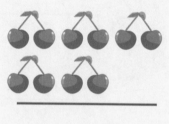

_____

- - - - - - - - -

_____

3

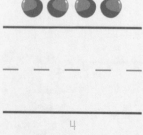

_____

- - - - - - - - -

_____

4

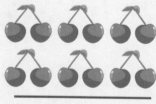
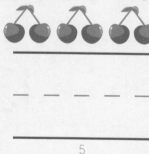

_____

- - - - - - - - -

_____

5

_____

- - - - - - - - -

_____

6

Pair Up

How many shoes does each person have? COUNT by twos to count the shoes.
Then WRITE the number.

1

2

3

4

Sandwich Slices

There are two slices of bread in each sandwich. COUNT by twos to count the slices of bread. Then WRITE the number.

_____

_ _ _ _ _

_____

1

_____

_ _ _ _ _

_____

2

_____

_ _ _ _ _

_____

3

_____

_ _ _ _ _

_____

4

_____

_ _ _ _ _

_____

5

_____

_ _ _ _ _

_____

6

Candy Count

CIRCLE groups of two jellybeans to help you count. Then WRITE the number of jellybeans.

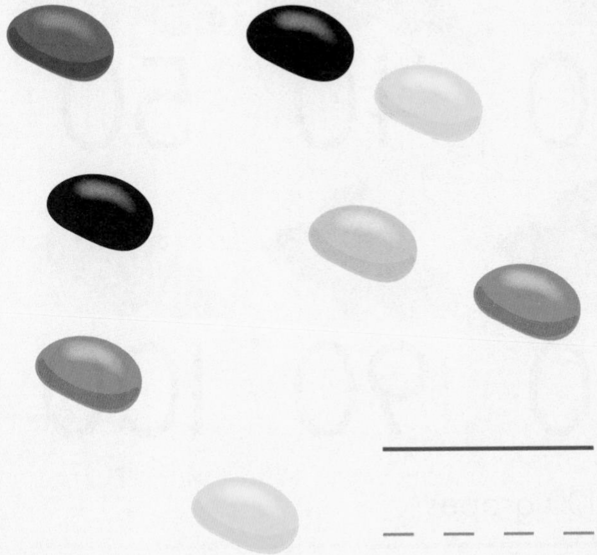

1

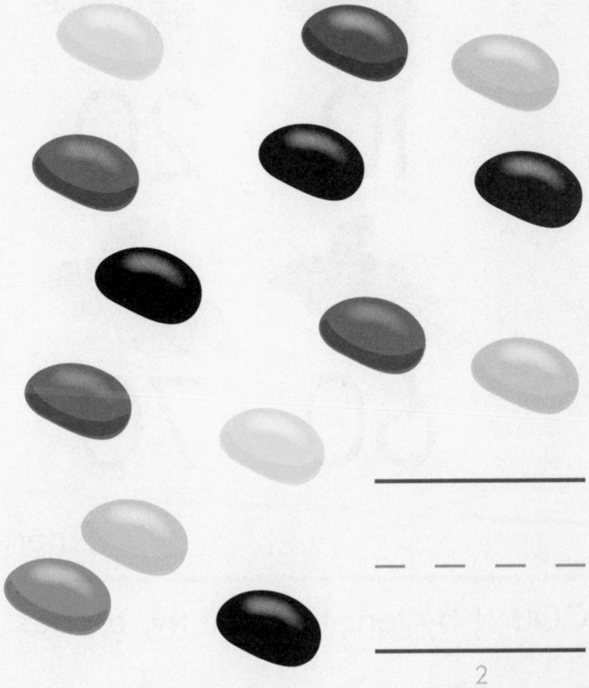

2

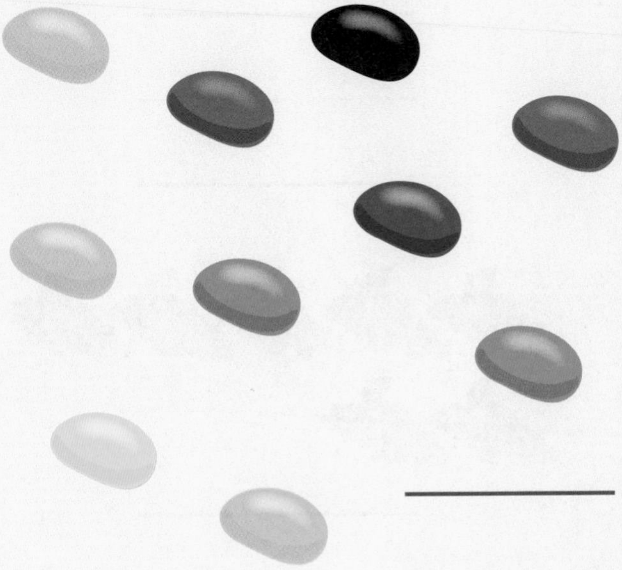

3

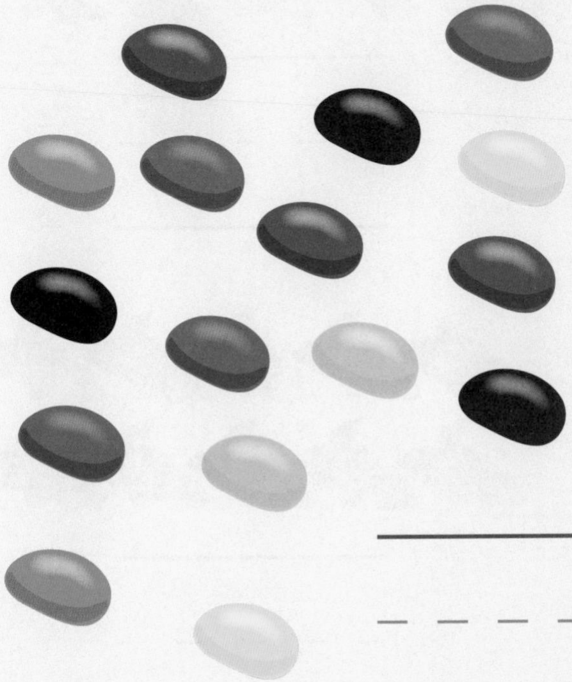

4

Great Grapes

There are 10 grapes in each bunch.

10   20   30   40   50

60   70   80   90   100

There are 100 grapes.

COUNT by tens to count the grapes. Then WRITE the number.

_____

- - - - - - - -

_____

1

_____

- - - - - - - -

_____

2

_____

- - - - - - - -

_____

3

_____

- - - - - - - -

_____

4

Hot Dog!

Hot dogs come in packages of 10. COUNT by tens to count the hot dogs. Then WRITE the number.

_____

_ _ _ _ _ _ _ _
1

_____

_ _ _ _ _ _ _ _
2

_____

_ _ _ _ _ _ _ _
3

_____

_ _ _ _ _ _ _ _
4

_____

_ _ _ _ _ _ _ _
5

_____

_ _ _ _ _ _ _ _
6

Counting by Tens

Enjoy the View

There are eight staircases to climb to the top of the hill to enjoy the view. Each staircase has 10 steps. COUNT by tens to count all the steps. Then WRITE the number of steps to get to the top of the hill.

_____

_ _ _ _ _ _ _ _

_____

Candy Count

CIRCLE groups of 10 jellybeans to help you count. Then WRITE the number of jellybeans.

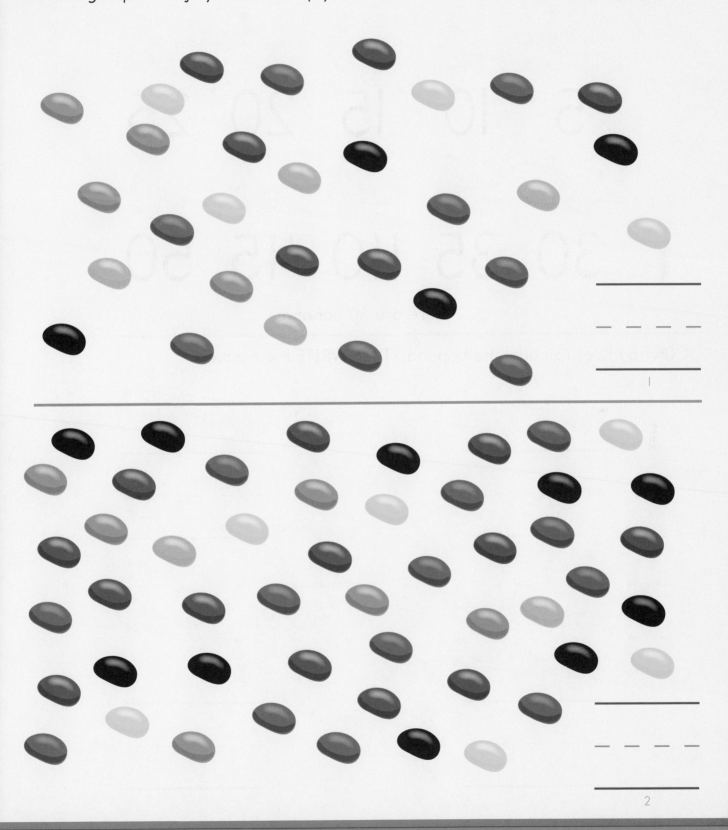

Counting by Fives

Going Bananas

There are five bananas in each bunch.

5   10   15   20   25

30   35   40   45   50

There are 50 bananas.

COUNT by fives to count the bananas. Then WRITE the number.

1

2

3

4

11

High Five

COUNT by fives to count the fingers. Then WRITE the number.

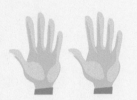

_____

- - - - - - - - -

_____ 1

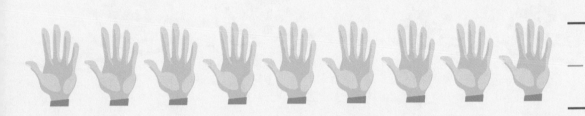

_____

- - - - - - - - -

_____ 2

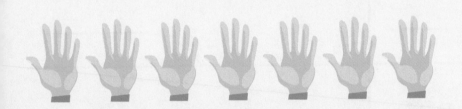

_____

- - - - - - - - -

_____ 3

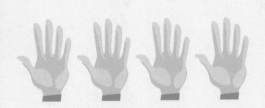

_____

- - - - - - - - -

_____ 4

_____

- - - - - - - - -

_____ 5

Alien Arms

Each alien has five arms. COUNT by fives to count the arms. Then WRITE the number of alien arms.

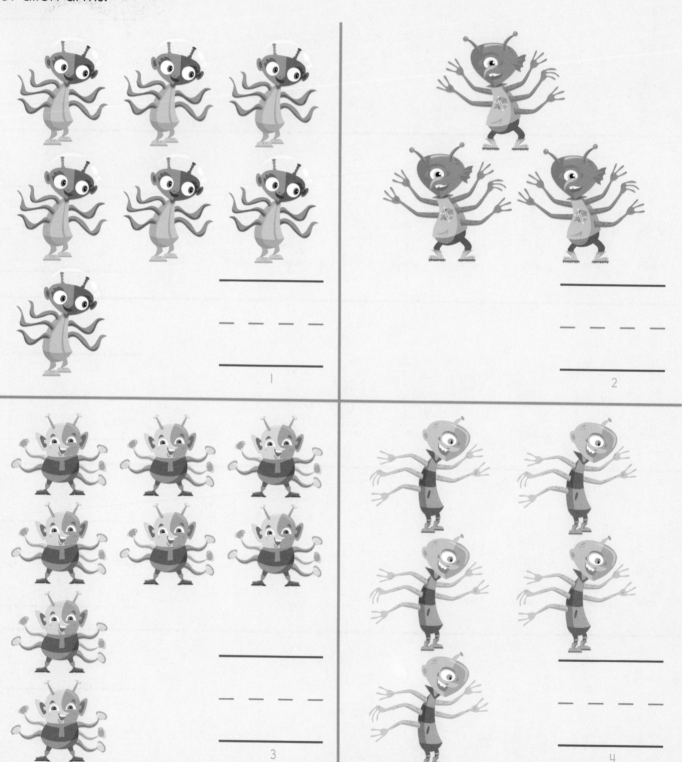

So Many Marbles

Each jar has five marbles. COUNT by fives to count the marbles. Then WRITE the number.

_____

– – – – – – –

_____

1

_____

– – – – – – –

_____

2

_____

– – – – – – –

_____

3

_____

– – – – – – –

_____

4

Windows on the Block

Each house has five windows. COUNT by fives to count the windows. Then WRITE the number of windows on each block.

1

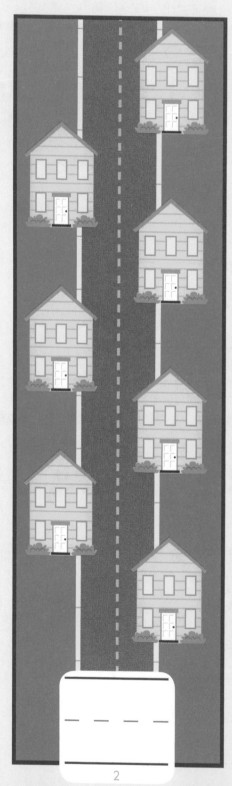

2

3

Candy Count

CIRCLE groups of five jellybeans to help you count. Then WRITE the number of jellybeans.

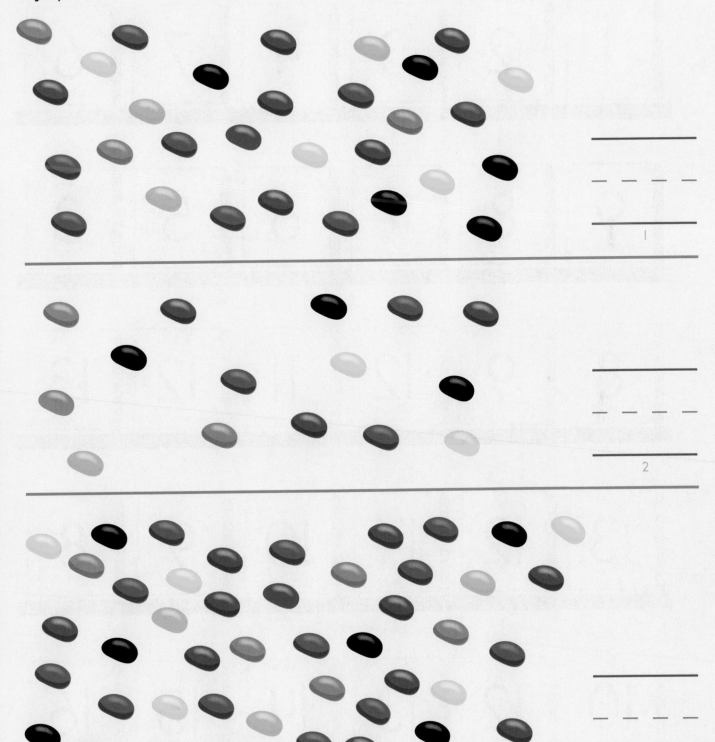

Shelf Switcheroo

There's one book out of place in each row. CIRCLE the book with the wrong number.

1. 1 2 3 4 7 6

2. 9 8 7 6 5 3

3. 8 9 12 11 12 13

4. 13 12 14 10 9 8

5. 10 12 13 14 15 16

Number Paths

WRITE the missing numbers to complete each pattern.

Path 1: ___, 2, 3, 4, ___, 6, 7, ___, 9

Path 2: 4, ___, 6, 7, ___, 10, 11, 12

Path 3: 6, 7, ___, 9, ___, 11, 12, ___, 14

Path 4: ___, 11, 12, 13, 14, ___, 16, 17, ___

Toys to Share

CIRCLE **even** or **odd** for each group.

1.

even

odd

2.

even

odd

3.

even

odd

4.

even

odd

5.

even

odd

Count by Twos

COUNT by twos to count the objects. Then WRITE the number.

1

2

3

4

5

93

Count by Tens

COUNT by tens to count the objects. Then WRITE the number.

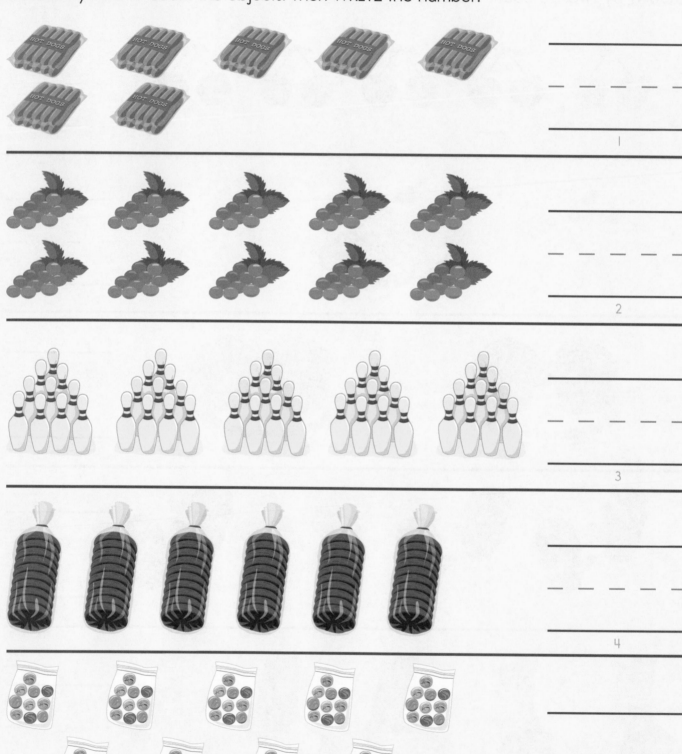

1 _____

2 _____

3 _____

4 _____

5 _____

Count by Fives

COUNT by fives to count the objects. Then WRITE the number.

_____

_ _ _ _ _ _ _ _ _ _

1

_____

_ _ _ _ _ _ _ _ _ _

2

_____

_ _ _ _ _ _ _ _ _ _

3

_____

_ _ _ _ _ _ _ _ _ _

4

_____

_ _ _ _ _ _ _ _ _ _

5

More or Less

Which Has More?

COUNT each group of balls. Then CIRCLE the group that has **more** than the other.

Frog Friends

COUNT the frogs on each lily pad, and WRITE the number. Then CIRCLE the numbers that are less than 4.

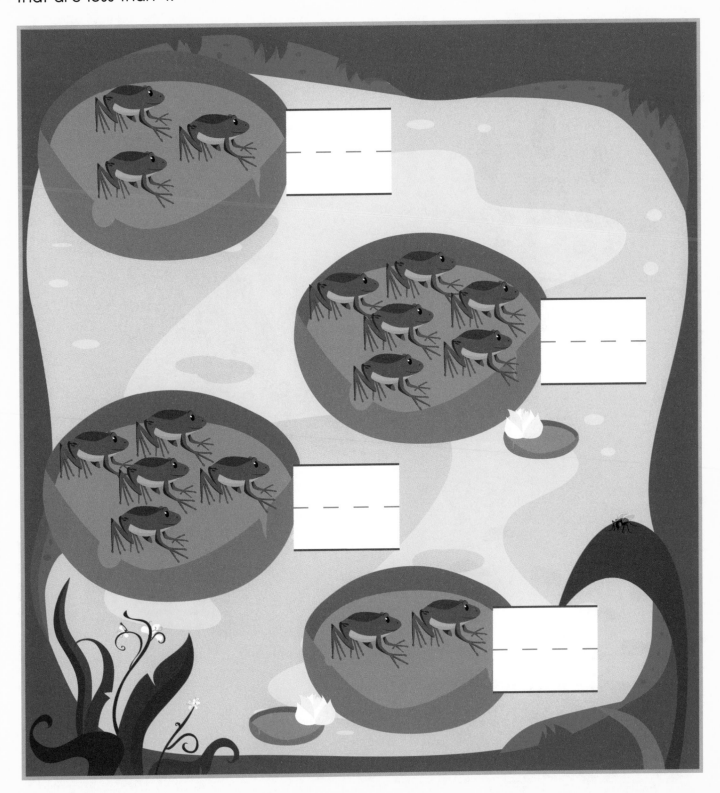

Royal Rings

COUNT the rings on each queen's hand. CIRCLE the hand that has **more** rings.

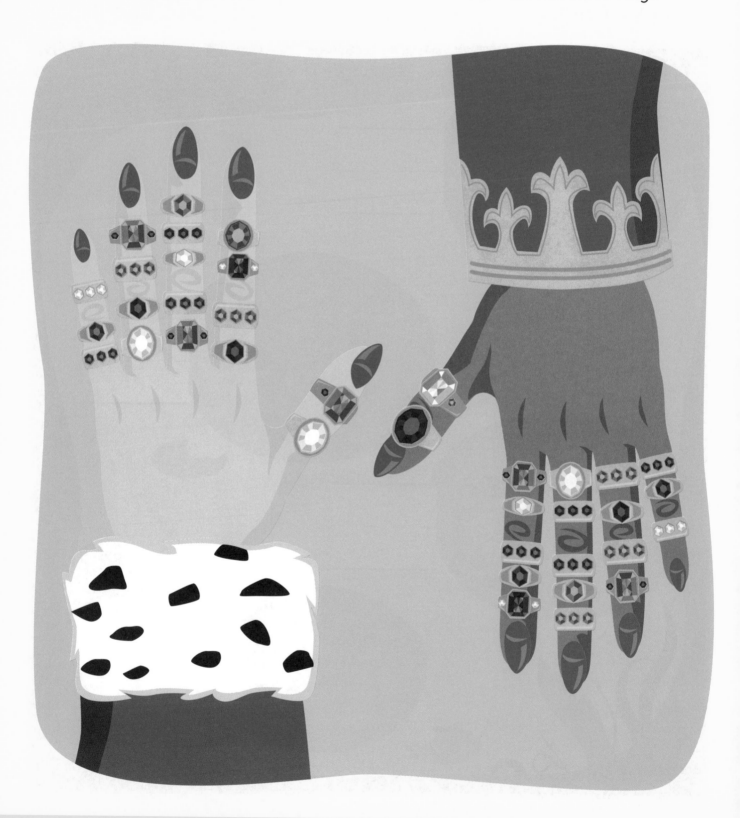

Chicken Coop

COUNT the eggs, and WRITE the number. Then CIRCLE the numbers that are less than 12.

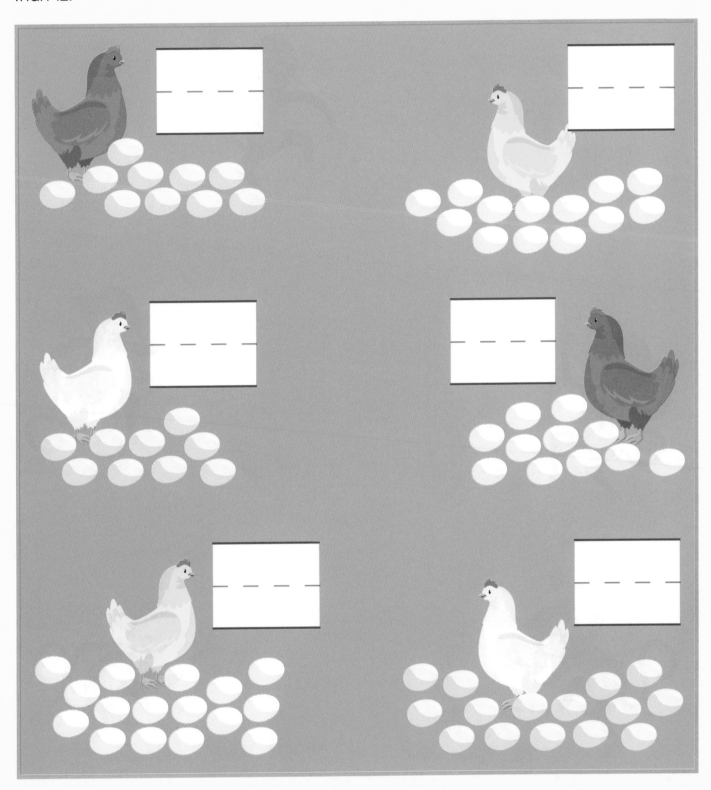

More or Less

More Bananas!

CIRCLE the monkeys that have **more** bananas than the top monkey.

Strawberry Fields

COUNT the strawberries on each plant, and WRITE the number. Then CIRCLE the numbers that are less than 16.

_____

- - - - - - - - -

_____

_____

- - - - - - - - -

_____

_____

- - - - - - - - -

_____

_____

- - - - - - - - -

_____

One More Book

CIRCLE the stack of books that has **one more** book than the first stack.

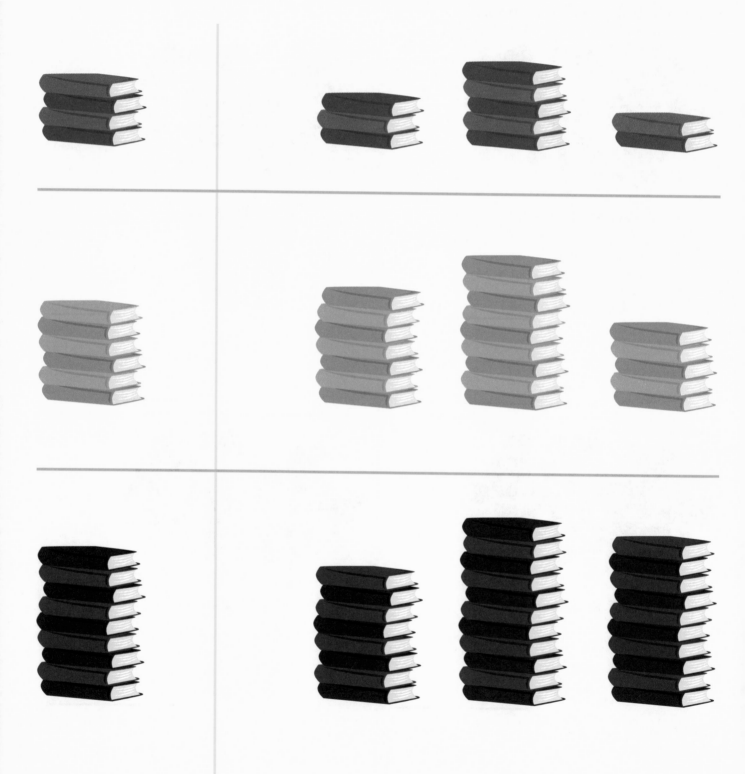

Can Do!

COUNT the cans in each stack, and WRITE the number. CIRCLE the number that is **one less** than the top number.

| 4 | 7 | 8 |

Guess and Check

Estimating is making a wise guess about the number of things in a group. GUESS the number of marbles in each group. Then CHECK your guess by counting the marbles.

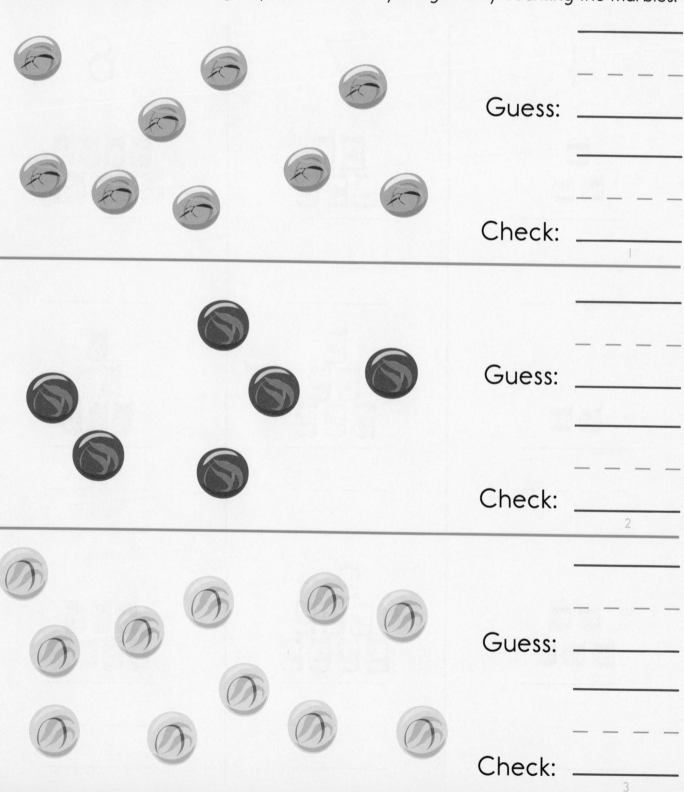

Guess: _____

Check: _____

Guess: _____

Check: _____

Guess: _____

Check: _____

_____

_ _ _ _ _ _ _ _

Guess: _____

_____

Check: _____
4

_____

_ _ _ _ _ _ _ _

Guess: _____

_____

Check: _____
5

_____

_ _ _ _ _ _ _ _

Guess: _____

_____

Check: _____
6

Blow Out the Candles

GUESS the number of candles on the cake. Then CHECK your guess by counting the candles.

Guess: _____ Check: _____

Perfect Ten

GUESS which row has 10 trophies, and CIRCLE it. Then COUNT the trophies to check your guess.

Estimating

Lucky Thirteen

GUESS which group has 13 horseshoes, and CIRCLE it. Then COUNT the horseshoes to check your guess.

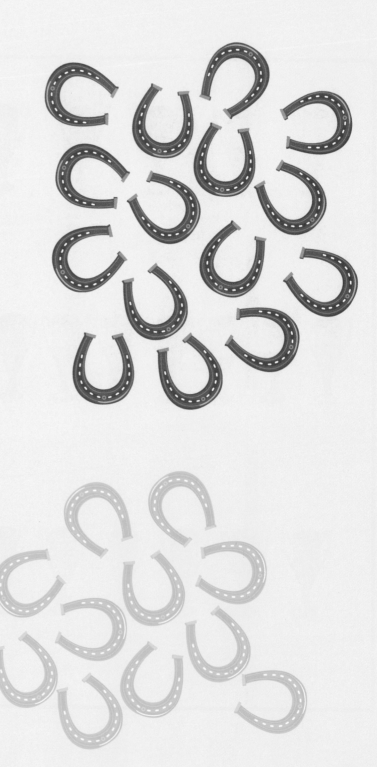

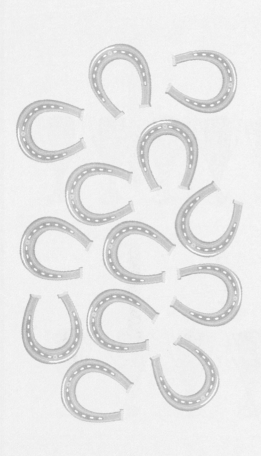

Gumball Guess

GUESS the number of gumballs in the gumball machine. Then CHECK your guess by counting the gumballs.

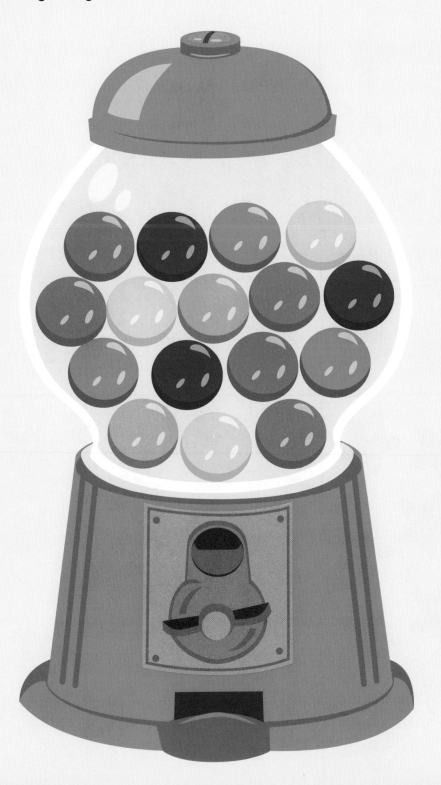

Guess: _____

Check: _____

Seeing Stars

GUESS which group has 17 stars, and CIRCLE it. Then COUNT the stars to check your guess.

Check the Crowd

GUESS the number of people in the picture. Then CHECK your guess by counting the people.

Guess: _____

Check: _____

Lemon Trees

COUNT the lemons on each tree, and WRITE the number. CIRCLE the numbers that are less than 8.

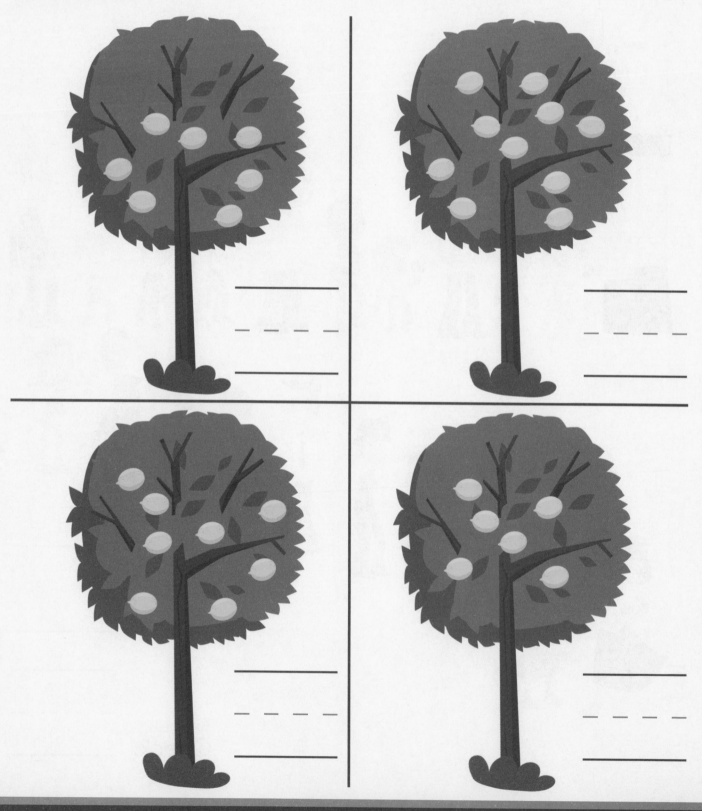

More Moons

COUNT the moons around each planet. CIRCLE the planet that has **more** moons than the other.

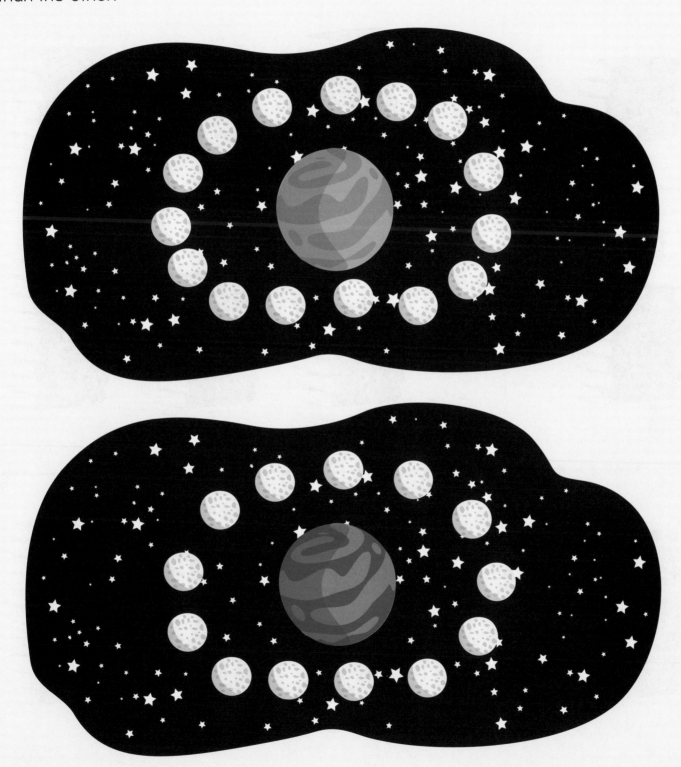

One More Book

CIRCLE the stack of books that has **one more** book than the first stack.

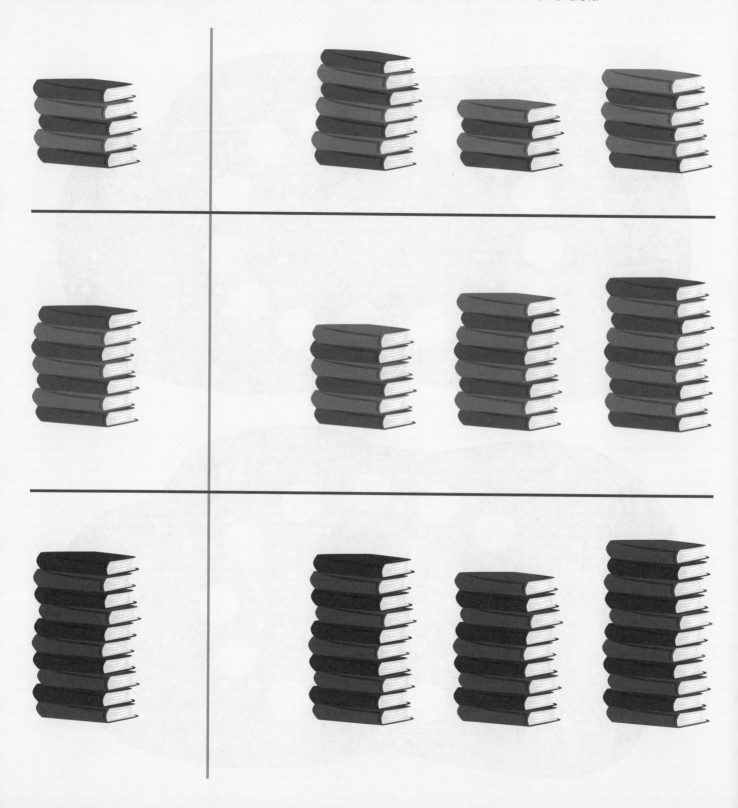

Guess and Check

GUESS the number of animals in each group. Then CHECK your guess by counting the animals.

Guess: _____

Check: _____

1

Guess: _____

Check: _____

2

Guess: _____

Check: _____

3

Lucky Ladybugs

GUESS which group has 15 ladybugs, and CIRCLE it. Then COUNT the ladybugs to check your guess.

Seeing Stars

GUESS the number of stars in each group. Then CHECK your guess by counting the stars.

Guess: _____

Check: _____

1

Guess: _____

Check: _____

2

Guess: _____

Check: _____

3

Answers

Page 2
Suggestion:

Page 3
Suggestion:

Page 4
Suggestion:

Page 5
Suggestion:
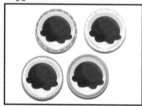

Page 6
Suggestion:

Page 7
Suggestion:

Page 8
Suggestion:

Page 9
Suggestion:

Page 10
Suggestion:

Page 11
Suggestion:
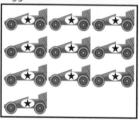

Page 12

Page 13
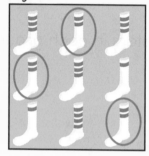

Page 14
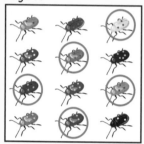

Page 15
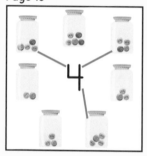

Page 16

Page 17
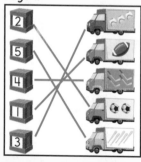

Page 18

Page 19
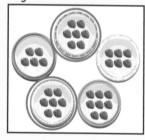

Page 20
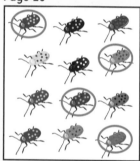

Page 21
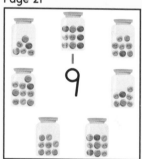

Page 22
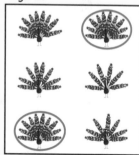

Page 23

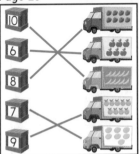

Page 24

Suggestion:

Page 25

Page 28

1. 4th
2. 5th
3. 1st
4. 6th
5. 3rd
6. 2nd

Page 29

1. 4th
2. 2nd
3. 6th
4. 8th

Page 30

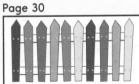

Page 31

1.  2.

3. 4.

5. 6.

Page 32

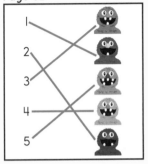

Page 33

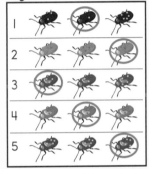

Page 34

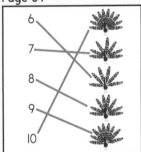

Page 35

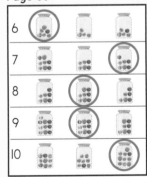

Page 36

Page 37

Page 38

Have someone check
your answers.

Page 39

Have someone check
your answers.

Page 40

Have someone check
your answers.

Page 41

Have someone check
your answers.

Page 42

Have someone check
your answers.

Page 43

Have someone check
your answers.

Page 44

Have someone check
your answers.

Page 45

Have someone check
your answers.

Page 46

Have someone check
your answers.

Page 47

Have someone check
your answers.

Page 48

Suggestion:

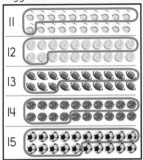

Page 49

1. 12
2. 13
3. 11

Page 50

1. 13
2. 15
3. 12
4. 16

Page 51

Suggestion:

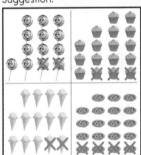

Page 52

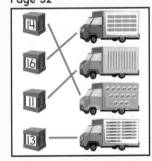

Page 53

Suggestion:

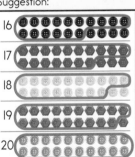

Answers

Page 54
1. 17 2. 14
3. 19

Page 55
1. 16 2. 20
3. 17 4. 18

Page 56
Suggestion:
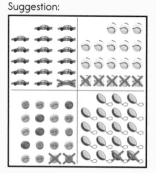

Page 57

Page 58
Suggestion:
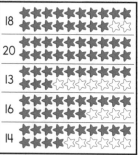

Page 59
Suggestion:
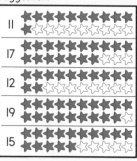

Page 60
1. 19 2. 15
3. 18

Page 61
Suggestion:
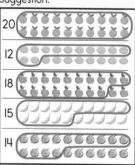

Page 62
Suggestion:
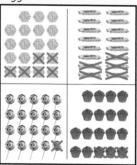

Page 63
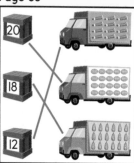

Page 64

Page 65
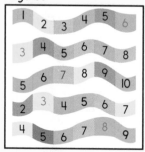

Page 66
8

6

7

9

1

Page 67
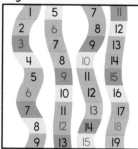

Page 68

Page 69

Page 70
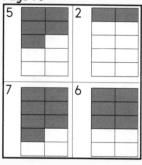

Page 71
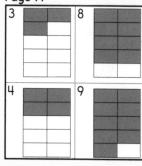

Page 72
1. odd 2. even
3. odd 4. even

Page 73

Page 74

120

Answers

Page 75

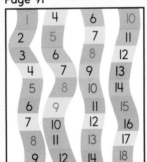

Page 76
1. 6   2. 14
3. 10   4. 8
5. 12   6. 20

Page 77
1. 10   2. 8
3. 18   4. 16

Page 78
1. 10   2. 6
3. 12   4. 14
5. 8   6. 18

Page 79
1. 8   2. 14
3. 10   4. 16

Page 80
1. 50   2. 20
3. 100   4. 70

Page 81
1. 40   2. 90
3. 10   4. 30
5. 80   6. 60

Page 82
80

Page 83
1. 30   2. 50

Page 84
1. 15   2. 25
3. 50   4. 35

Page 85
1. 10   2. 45
3. 35   4. 20
5. 30

Page 86
1. 35   2. 15
3. 40   4. 25

Page 87
1. 40   2. 30
3. 50   4. 45

Page 88
1. 25   2. 35
3. 20

Page 89
1. 30   2. 15
3. 45

Page 90
1. 7
2. 3
3. 12
4. 14
5. 10

Page 91

Page 92
1. even   2. even
3. odd   4. odd
5. even

Page 93
1. 10   2. 6
3. 4   4. 8
5. 10

Page 94
1. 70   2. 100
3. 50   4. 60
5. 90

Page 95
1. 45   2. 50
3. 30   4. 15
5. 35

Page 96

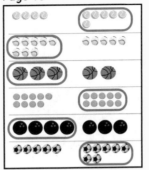

Page 97

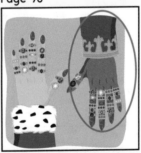

Page 98

Page 99

Page 100

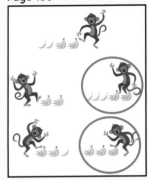

Page 101

Page 102

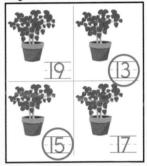

Page 103

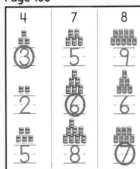

Pages 104–105
Check:
1. 9   2. 6
3. 11   4. 15
5. 7   6. 13

Answers

Page 106
Check: 8

Page 107

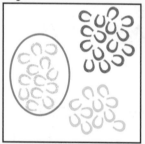

Page 108

Page 109
Check: 16

Page 110

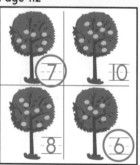

Page 111
Check: 20

Page 112

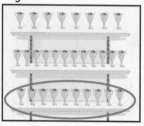

Page 113

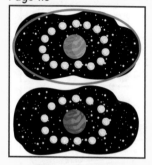

Page 114

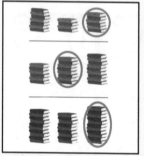

Page 115
Check:
  1. 8   2. 14
3. 19

Page 116

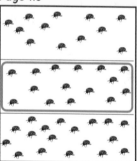

Page 117
Check:
  1. 15   2. 20
3. 18

Kindergarten
Success with Sight Words

Contents

Jiffy Words

Space Trace

Space Ace found words in the stars! TRACE the words so he can read them.

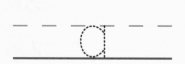 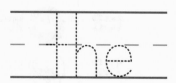 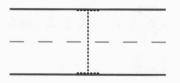

Say It

LOOK at the words. READ each word out loud. Then READ each word out loud again in a super-quiet voice.

Jiffy Words

Spot the Dots

READ each word in the box. LOOK for only those words in the picture. DRAW a line to connect the words in ABC order, as they appear in the box. FIND the mystery picture!

HINT: It is crunchy and sweet and good to eat.

a	am	are	I	is	the

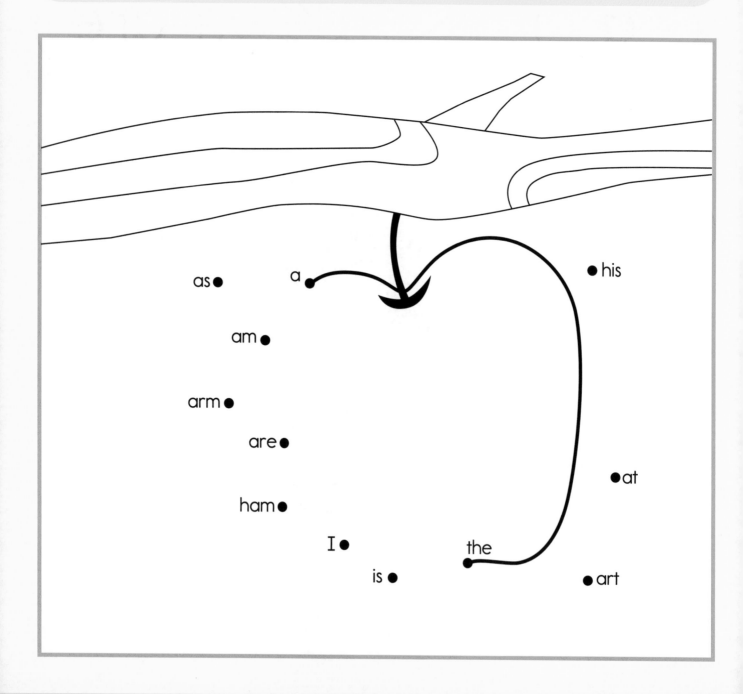

Word Blocks

SAY the words. FILL IN each word block with a word of the same shape.

a   am   are   I   is   the

1.

2.

3.

4.

5.

6.

Blank Out

READ each word. LOOK at each picture. WRITE the word to complete each sentence.

HINT: Each word is used only once.

am	are	a	is

I see _____ blue bird.
1

The flower _____ red.
2

The balloons _____ green.
3

I _____ in the bed.
4

Start Your Crayons!

READ the words. COLOR only the dinosaurs that are wearing the words from the box.

a   the   I   am   is   are

Blank Out

READ each word. LOOK at each picture. WRITE the word to complete each sentence.

HINT: Each word is used only once.

| see | find | run | come | can |

I _____ fast.
1

The pig _____ fly!
2

Do not let the dog _____ in.
3

Help me _____ my shoe.
4

I _____ a bear.
5

Poetry Guy

Help Poetry Guy write his poems. READ the words. FILL IN words that rhyme.

come	see	run	can

It is lots of fun

to _____.
    1

I can _____
        2

a busy bee.

Will you _____?
            3

I have some gum!

My hat _____
        4

fit in a pan.

Match It

READ each word. DRAW a line from each word to the correct picture.

find

see

run

come

Story Time

READ the words. Then READ the story. CIRCLE the words as you find them.

can	see	run	come	find

I come home from school.

I run into the house.

I see a box!

I find my name on it.

Yay!

I can open the box!

Word Hunt

READ the words. CIRCLE the words in the grid. WRITE each word after you circle it. Words go across and down.

run	see	can	find	come

i	q	r	c	f
s	s	u	o	i
c	a	n	m	n
s	e	e	e	d

Meet in the Middle

Can you help these kids get to the middle of the maze? READ the word each kid is wearing. FIND the words in the maze. DRAW a line through the words to get to the middle.

Space Trace

Space Ace found words in the stars! TRACE the words so he can read them.

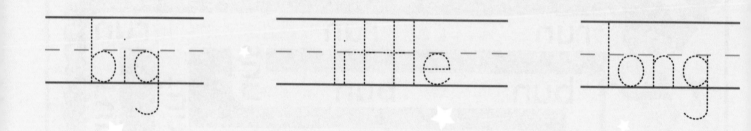

big   little   long

old   pretty

Start Your Crayons!

READ the words. COLOR only the dinosaurs that are wearing the words from the box.

big	little	long	old	pretty

What's It Like?

Blank Out

READ each word. LOOK at each picture. WRITE the word to complete each sentence.

HINT: Each word is used only once.

| big | little | long | pretty |

The elephant is _____.
1

The mouse is very _____.
2

The flower is _____.
3

The line is very _____.
4

Stop, Drop, and Draw

READ each sentence. DRAW a picture to match each sentence.

Here is a pretty bird.

That is a big shoe!

Look at the long snake.

See the old house.

Word Hunt

READ the words. CIRCLE the words in the grid. WRITE each word after you circle it.
Words go across and down.

| is | old | see | come | run | big | am | long |

```
i  o  l  d  s
s  c  o  m  e
r  u  n  a  e
b  i  g  m  f
```

Word Blocks

SAY the words. FILL IN each word block with a word of the same shape.

the   find   can   little   pretty   I

1.

2.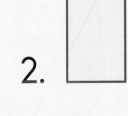

3.

4.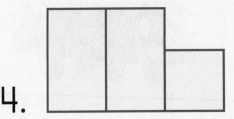

5.

6.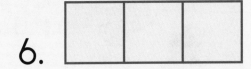

Colorful Words

Hide and Speak

READ each color word out loud. DRAW a line from each color word to a car in the picture that matches it.

red   blue   yellow   green   brown   black

Pink

Name It

LOOK at each picture. READ the words next to the picture. CIRCLE the word that matches the picture.

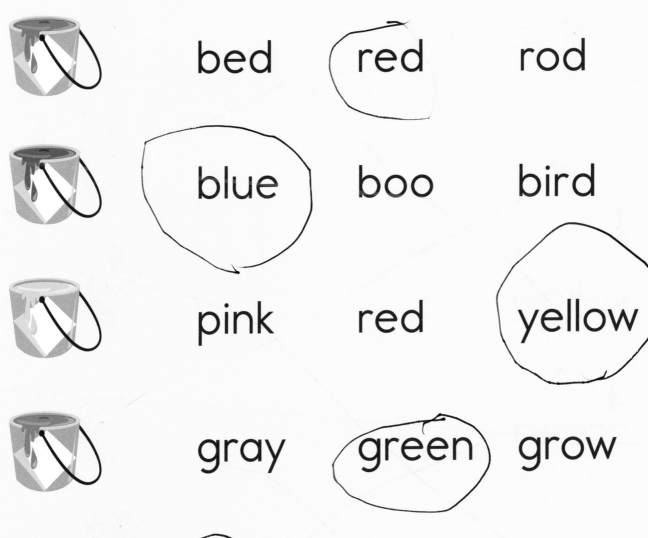

bed   (red)   rod

(blue)   boo   bird

pink   red   (yellow)

gray   (green)   grow

(brown)   bow   town

back   block   (black)

Colorful Words

Match It

READ each word. DRAW a line from each word to the correct picture.

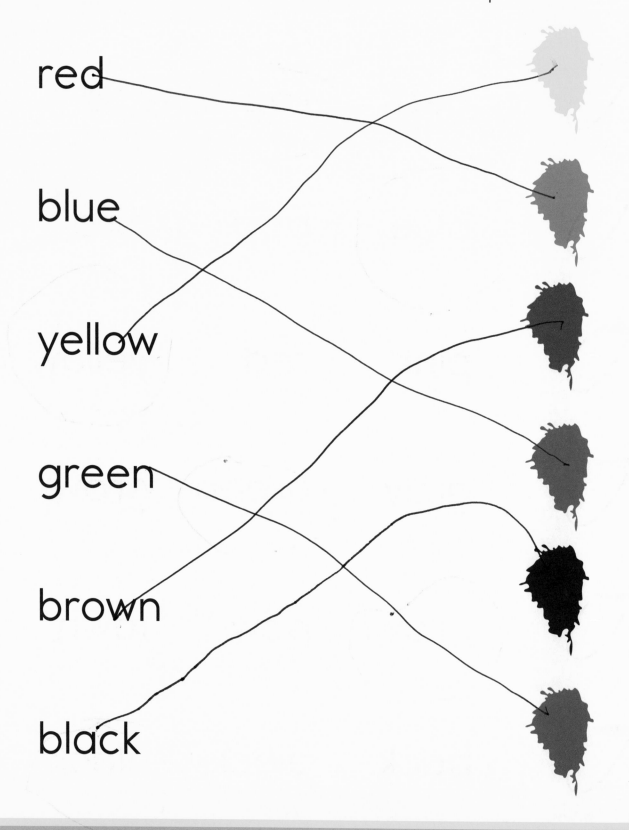

red

blue

yellow

green

brown

black

4

Blank Out

READ each word. LOOK at each picture. WRITE the word to complete each sentence.

red   blue   yellow   green   brown   black

I see a __blue__ bird.
1

My dress is __red__ .
2

Here is a __black__ horse.
3

I love the __yellow__ sun.
4

The leaf is __green__ .
5

The bug is __brown__ .
6

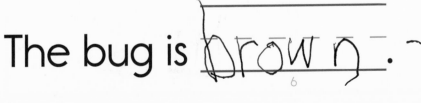

Colorful Words

Start Your Crayons!

READ the words. COLOR only the dinosaurs that are wearing the words from the box—and make the colors match the words too!

red   blue   yellow   green   brown   black

Stop, Drop, and Draw

READ each sentence. DRAW a picture to match each sentence.

I have a green hat.

She has blue shoes.

The fish is red.

I see a brown bear.

Tag It

TRACE the words. DRAW a line from each word to the animal it matches in the picture.

dog   cat   bird

rabbit   fish

Name It

LOOK at each picture. READ the words next to the picture. CIRCLE the word that matches the picture.

 dig (dog) hog

 (cat) cut rat

 robot (rabbit) rub

 bad bat (bird)

 (fish) dish fun

Story Time

READ the words. Then READ the story. CIRCLE the words as you find them.

| cat | dog | fish | bird | rabbit |

The dog took a bath.

The cat took a bath.

So did the rabbit.

The bird did too.

"Please get out of my bowl," said the fish.

Match It

READ each word. DRAW a line from each word to the correct picture.

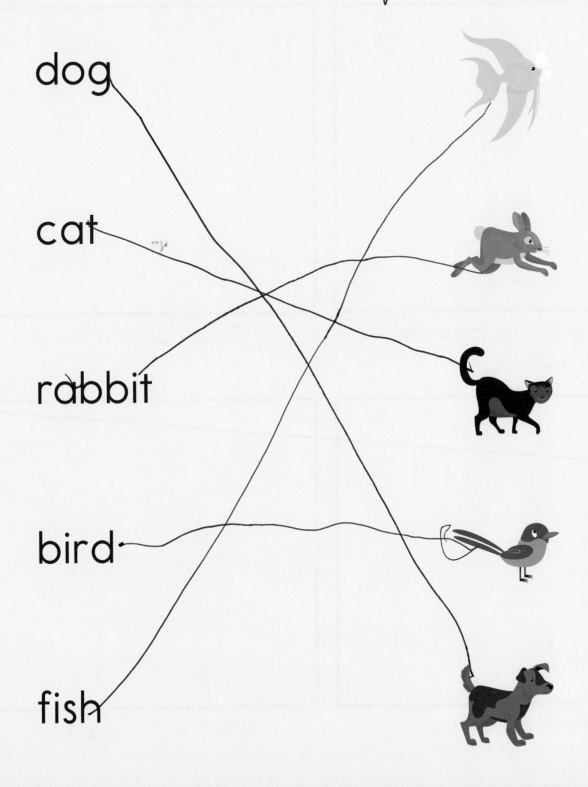

dog

cat

rabbit

bird

fish

Stop, Drop, and Draw

READ each sentence. DRAW a picture to match each sentence.

My dog has long ears.

That cat can fly.

I see a green rabbit.

A fish is in my bed!

Spot the Dots

READ each word in the box. LOOK for only those words in the picture. DRAW a line to connect the words in ABC order, as they appear in the box. FIND the mystery picture!

HINT: This little pet likes to get wet.

| bird | cat | dog | fish | rabbit |

dish

dig

rat

mat

dog

dug

fish

cat

rabbit

bud

bird

wish

Space Trace

Space Ace found words in the stars! TRACE the words so he can read them.

at

not

to

an

will

say

Say It

LOOK at the words. READ each word out loud. Then READ each word out loud again, but this time clap after each word.

Word Blocks

SAY the words. FILL IN each word block with a word of the same shape.

| at | not | to | an | will | say |

1.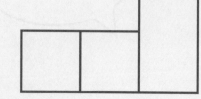

2.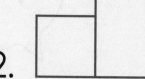

3.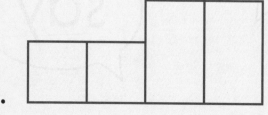

4.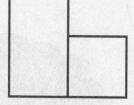

5.

6.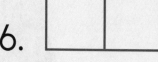

Blank Out

READ each word. LOOK at each picture. WRITE the word to complete each sentence.

HINT: Each word is used only once.

will	to	not	an

I do _____ like rain.
1

He gave the box _____ the girl.
2

The baby _____ cry if you go.
3

The boy ate _____ apple.
4

Start Your Crayons!

READ the words. COLOR only the dinosaurs that are wearing the words from the box.

at	not	to	an	will	say

Meet in the Middle

Can you help these kids get to the middle of the maze? READ the word each kid is wearing. FIND the words in the maze. DRAW a line through the words to get to the middle.

Space Trace

Space Ace found words in the stars! TRACE the words so he can read them.

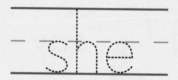

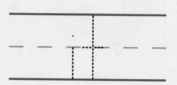

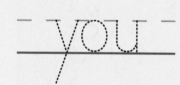

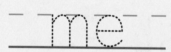

Word Blocks

SAY the words. FILL IN each word block with a word of the same shape.

he   she   it   you   me

1.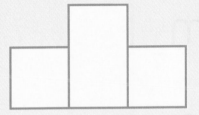

2.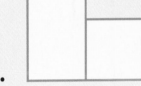

3.

4.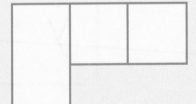

5.

Word Hunt

READ the words. CIRCLE the words in the grid. WRITE each word after you circle it. Words go across and down.

he   she   it   you   me   we

i	t	m
s	h	e
w	e	r
y	o	u

Spot the Dots

READ each word in the box. LOOK for only those words in the picture. DRAW a line to connect the words in ABC order, as they appear in the box. FIND the mystery picture!

HINT: You and me—we need this for tea!

he   it   me   she   we   you

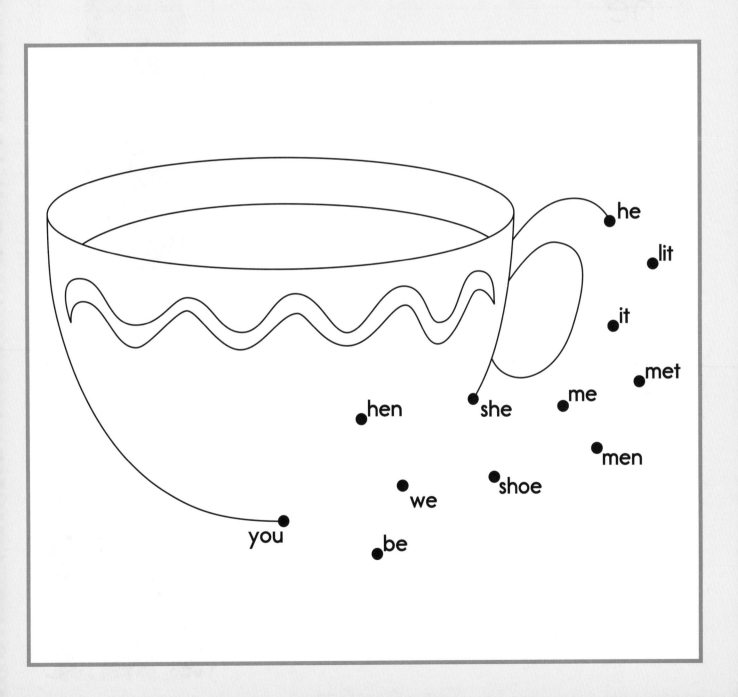

Match It

READ each word. DRAW a line from each word to the correct picture.

he

it

she

we

Meet in the Middle

Can you help these kids get to the middle of the maze? READ the word each kid is wearing. FIND the words in the maze. DRAW a line through the words to get to the middle.

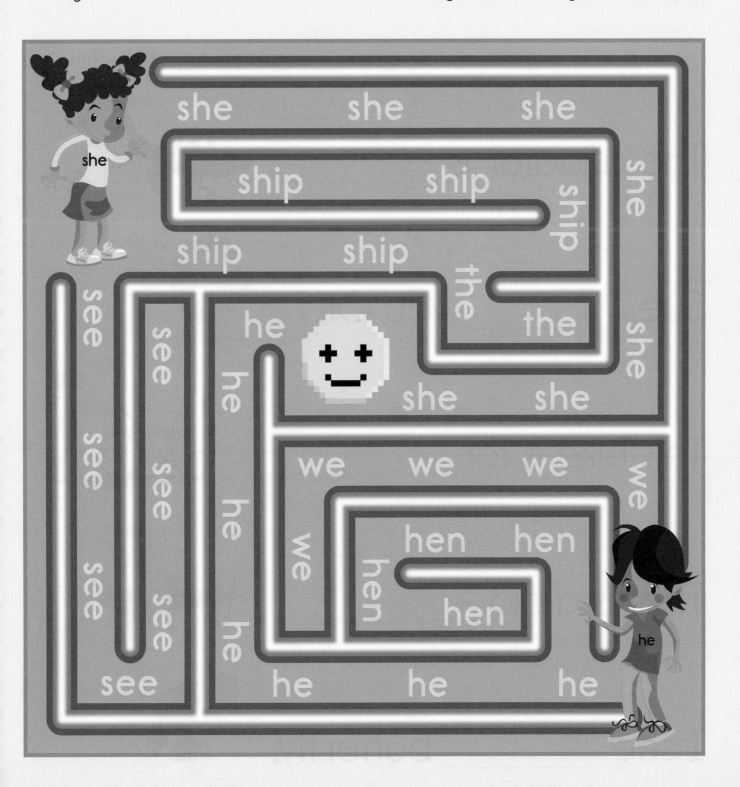

Blank Out

READ each word. LOOK at each picture. WRITE the word to complete each sentence.

HINT: Each word is used only once.

a	you	are	green	fish

The alligator is _____.
1

Sue, _____ you OK?
2

This bike is for _____.
3

That is a big _____.
4

I see _____ butterfly.
5

Try to Remember

CUT OUT the cards. READ the rules. PLAY the game!

Rules: Two players
1. MIX UP the cards.
2. PLACE the cards face down on a table.
3. TAKE TURNS turning over two cards at a time.
4. KEEP the cards when you match two words.

How many matches can you collect?

me	me	he	he
are	are	an	an
you	you	will	will
to	to	the	the

he	he	me	me
an	an	are	are
will	will	you	you
the	the	to	to

Word Hunt

READ the words. CIRCLE the words in the grid. WRITE each word after you circle it.
Words go across and down.

rabbit   not   say   you   green   are   big   she

```
x   g   r   e   e   n
a   s   h   e   b   o
r   a   b   b   i   t
e   y   o   u   g   m
```

Match It

READ each word. DRAW a line from each word to the correct number.

five

six

two

four

one

three

1

2

3

4

5

6

Name It

LOOK at each number. READ the words next to the number. CIRCLE the word that matches the number.

1   won   one   on

2   to   top   two

3   three   tree   two

4   for   fur   four

5   hive   five   fit

6   six   sick   sacks

Count on It!

Blank Out

READ each word. LOOK at each picture. WRITE the word to complete each sentence.

HINT: Each word is used only once.

| one | two | three | four | five | six |

The doll has _____ shoes.
1

An ant has _____ legs.
2

I blew _____ bubble.
3

The giraffe has _____ legs.
4

A hand has _____ fingers.
5

Here are _____ paintbrushes.
6

Spot the Dots

READ each word in the box. LOOK for only those words in the picture. DRAW a line to connect the words in 1-2-3 order to find the mystery picture.

HINT: This thing can ring—and even sing!

| one | two | three | four | five | six |

two

tow

tree

one

for

fur

three

too

six

four

sits

hive

five

Hooray for Play!

Tag It

TRACE the words. DRAW a line from each word to something it matches in the picture.

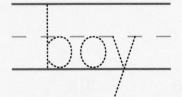

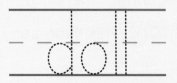

Start Your Crayons!

READ the words. COLOR only the dinosaurs that are wearing the words from the box.

boy	girl	toy	doll	ball

Hooray for Play!

Blank Out

READ each word. LOOK at each picture. WRITE the word to complete each sentence.

HINT: Each word is used only once.

boy	girl	toy	doll	ball

The _____ has green hair.

1

A _____ is round.

2

See the _____ jump.

3

The _____ yells.

4

A top is a kind of _____.

5

Spot the Dots

READ each word in the box. LOOK for only those words in the picture. DRAW a line to connect the words in ABC order, as they appear in the box. FIND the mystery picture!

HINT: This one likes to play all day!

| ball | boy | doll | girl | toy |

bay

buy

ball

fall

gill

boy

doll

wall

girl

toy

roll

Say It

LOOK at the words. READ each word out loud. Then READ each word out loud again in a funny voice.

Word Blocks

SAY the words. FILL IN each word block with a word of the same shape.

go	get	play	ride	work

1.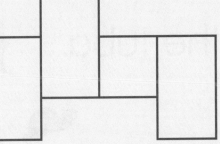

2.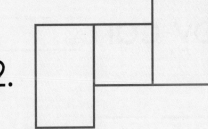

3.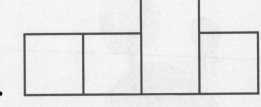

4.

5.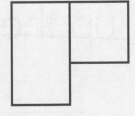

More Busy Words

Blank Out

READ each word. LOOK at each picture. WRITE the word to complete each sentence.

HINT: Each word is used only once.

| go | get | play | ride | work |

The boy can _____ the tuba.
1

I will _____ the red hat.
2

I _____ up the hill.
3

This is hard _____ !
4

See the girl _____ the horse.
5

Poetry Guy

Help Poetry Guy write his poems. READ the words. FILL IN words that rhyme.

get	ride	go	play

Will you _____
1

to see the show?

I like to _____
2

every day.

You will _____
3

very wet!

I do not _____
4

a horse inside.

Match It

READ each word. DRAW a line from each word to the correct picture.

go

ride

play

work

Meet in the Middle

Can you help these kids get to the middle of the maze? READ the word each kid is wearing. FIND the words in the maze. DRAW a line through the words to get to the middle.

Order Up!

MATCH each picture with a sentence. WRITE the number of the picture next to the sentence it matches. Now READ the story in the correct order.

1.

2.

3.

4.

Now we can play!

Get the brown rabbit.

Get the red toy.

Get the big ball.

Story Time

READ the words. Then READ the story. CIRCLE the words as you find them.

ball	boy	will	say	cat	toy	dog
rabbit	fish	girl	big	play	little	

The little girl has a rabbit.

The boy has a toy.

The big dog has a ball.

The cat has a fish.

"Will you play?" they say.

Yes!

Tag It

TRACE the words. DRAW a line from each word to the part of the picture it matches.

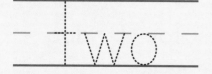  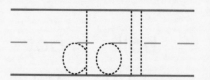

two   three   doll

MARBLES
JUST 5 CENTS!

RACE
CARS
2 FOR
3
DOLLARS!

ROARING
RACETRACK

ball   girl   five

Word Hunt

READ the words. CIRCLE the words in the grid. WRITE each word after you circle it.
Words go across and down.

boy   two   toy   doll   play   get   go   red   six   she

s	i	x	r	e	d
h	g	e	t	w	o
e	o	b	o	y	l
p	l	a	y	l	l

Even More Busy Words

Say It

LOOK at the words. READ each word out loud. Then READ each word out loud again in a "parrot" voice. Squawk!

Blank Out

READ each word. LOOK at each picture. WRITE the word to complete each sentence.

HINT: Each word is used only once.

give	want	like	look	make

See Dad _____ a cake.
   1

I will _____ you some pizza.
   2

I _____ in the mirror!
   3

I _____ my cat.
   4

Do you _____ some mud?
   5

Start Your Crayons!

READ the words. COLOR only the dinosaurs that are wearing the words from the box.

give   want   like   look   make

Word Blocks

SAY the words. FILL IN each word block with a word of the same shape.

| give | want | look | like | make |

1.

2.

3.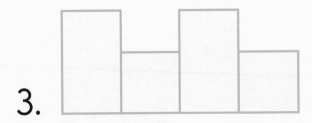

4.

5.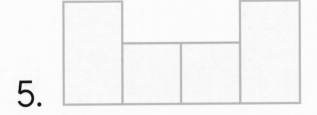

Match It

READ each word. DRAW a line from each word to the correct picture.

egg

cake

milk

soup

banana

apple

Hide and Speak

READ each word out loud. DRAW a line from each word to a food in the kitchen that matches it.

egg   cake   milk   soup   banana   apple

Order Up!

MATCH each picture with a sentence. WRITE the number of the picture next to the sentence it matches. Now READ the story in the correct order.

He put in milk.

Look! A cake!

I put in an egg.

She put in a banana.

Stop, Drop, and Draw

READ each sentence. DRAW a picture to match each sentence.

The cake is pretty.

Look what was in the egg.

A worm is in the apple.

This is birthday soup.

Tag It

TRACE the words. DRAW a line from each word to something it matches in the picture.

egg   cake   milk

soup   banana   apple

Name It

LOOK at each picture. READ the words next to the picture. CIRCLE the word that matches the picture.

  soap   soup   soak

  apple   ape   happy

 mint   melt   milk

  cook   make   cake

 egg   leg   edge

band   banana   bandage

Say It

LOOK at the words. READ each word out loud. Then READ each word out loud again, stopping each time to act it out before reading the next word.

up

on

in

down

out

under

Word Blocks

SAY the words. FILL IN each word block with a word of the same shape.

| up | down | on | under | out |

1.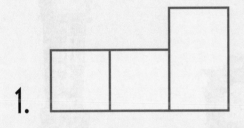

2.

3.

4.

5.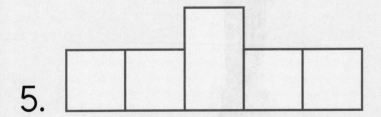

Where Is It?

Match It

READ each word. DRAW a line from each word to the correct picture.

HINT: To find the answer, look for the mouse in each picture.

up

down

in

under

Blank Out

READ each word. LOOK at each picture. WRITE the word to complete each sentence.

HINT: Each word is used only once.

up	down	in	on	under

The boy went _____ the hill.
1

The ball is _____ the dog.
2

The bug is _____ the net.
3

The cat is _____ the mitten.
4

The van went _____ the hill.
5

Where Is It?

Meet in the Middle

Can you help these kids get to the middle of the maze? READ the word each kid is wearing. FIND the words in the maze. DRAW a line through the words to get to the middle.

Order Up!

MATCH each picture with a sentence. WRITE the number of the picture next to the sentence it matches. Now READ the story in the correct order.

The turtle went in the water.

The turtle stuck out his head to say "Good-bye!"

The turtle went under the water.

The bird sat on the turtle.

Name It

LOOK at each picture. READ the words next to the picture. CIRCLE the word that matches the picture.

live   give   go

town   dawn   down

look   lock   book

up   pup   under

make   cake   cook

Try to Remember

CUT OUT the cards. READ the rules. PLAY the game!

Rules: Two players
1. MIX UP the cards.
2. PLACE the cards face down on a table.
3. TAKE TURNS turning over two cards at a time.
4. KEEP the cards when you match two words.

How many matches can you collect?

under	under	soup	soup
want	want	like	like
in	in	on	on
give	give	out	out

Poetry Guy

Help Poetry Guy write his poems. READ the words. FILL IN words that rhyme.

like	make	look	under

Can you _____ ₁

an apple cake?

Please take a _____ ₂

at my poetry book!

What is _____ ₃

this rock, I wonder!

I really _____ ₄

to ride my bike.

This & That

Say It

LOOK at the words. READ each word out loud. Then READ each word out loud again in a squeaky mouse voice.

Space Trace

Space Ace found words in the stars! TRACE the words so he can read them.

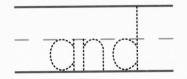

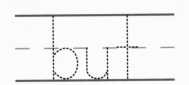

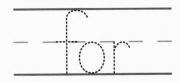

Word Blocks

SAY the words. FILL IN each word block with a word of the same shape.

| and | but | for | no | yes |

1.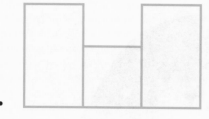

2.

3.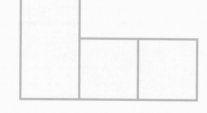

4.

5.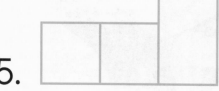

Start Your Crayons!

READ the words. COLOR only the dinosaurs that are wearing the words from the box.

| and | but | for | so | yes | no |

Space Trace

Space Ace found words in the stars! TRACE the words so he can read them.

do

has

have

was

my

be

Blank Out

READ each word. LOOK at each picture. WRITE the word to complete each sentence.

HINT: Each word is used only once.

| have | be | has | my | do |

I _____ not like big bugs.

₁

I _____ three snakes.

₂

She _____ a hot dog.

₃

This is _____ dog.

₄

Will you _____ my friend?

₅

Match It

READ each sentence. DRAW a line from each sentence to the correct picture.

I have four legs.

She has a doll.

I do not have fur.

Yes, my bird is green.

Poetry Guy

Help Poetry Guy write his poems. READ the words. FILL IN words that rhyme.

do	was	my	be

What can you _____
1

with a kangaroo?

You can have _____
2

apple pie.

My dog likes to _____
3

with me.

What bug _____
4

going "buzz, buzz, buzz"?

Spot the Dots

READ each word in the box. LOOK for only those words in the picture. DRAW a line to connect the words in ABC order, as they appear in the box. FIND the mystery picture!

HINT: I have wings but do not fly. My tummy is white. What am I?

| be | do | has | have | my | was |

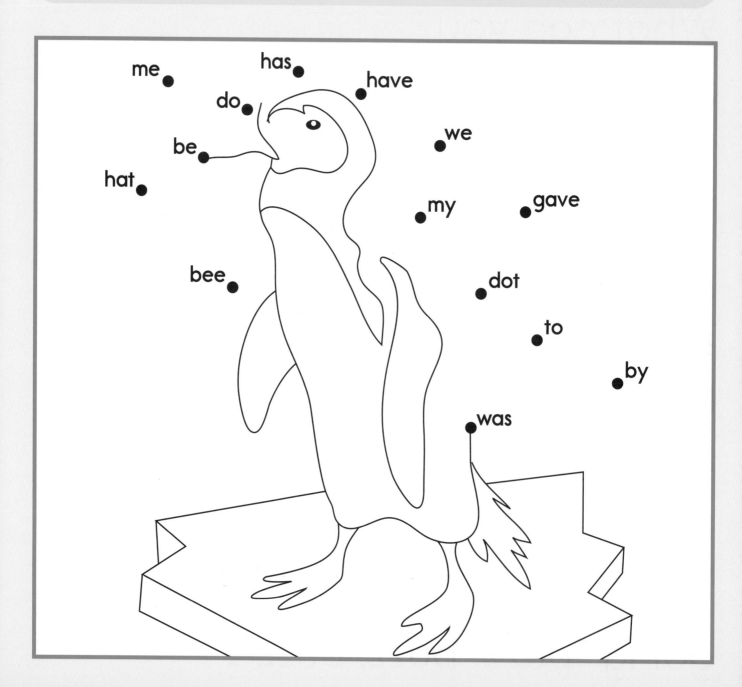

Meet in the Middle

Can you help these kids get to the middle of the maze? READ the word each kid is wearing. FIND the words in the maze. DRAW a line through the words to get to the middle.

Head to Toe

Tag It

TRACE the words. DRAW a line from each word to something it matches in the picture.

Name It

LOOK at each picture. READ the words next to the picture. CIRCLE the word that matches the picture.

 foot (feet) fee

 (leg) log beg

 I (eyes) yes

 band had (hand)

 (head) had hid

Order Up!

MATCH each picture with a sentence. WRITE the number of the picture next to the sentence it matches. Now READ the story in the correct order.

But only one hand!

I see a head.

I see lots of feet.

I see eyes.

Blank Out

READ each word. LOOK at each picture. WRITE the word to complete each sentence.

HINT: Each word is used only once.

| feet | leg | eyes | hand | head |

I have two _____.
1

My _____ is wet.
2

I hurt my _____
3

The cat has four _____.
4

The boy waves his _____.
5

Head to Toe

Story Time

READ the words. Then READ the story. CIRCLE the words as you find them.

| feet | leg | eyes | hand | head |

The dog licked my hand.

He sat by my feet.

Then he put his head on my leg.

I looked at his big brown eyes.

I will ask Dad if we can keep him!

Word Hunt

READ the words. CIRCLE the words in the grid. WRITE each word after you circle it. Words go across and down.

| feet | head | leg | eyes | hand |

f	m	l	e	h
e	y	e	s	e
e	h	g	a	a
t	h	a	n	d

225

Match It

READ each word. DRAW a line from each word to the correct picture.

100%

car

bus

boat

truck

train

plane

Stop, Drop, and Draw

READ each sentence. DRAW a picture to match each sentence.

This car can fly!

I sail my boat.

It's the ice cream truck!

Here is a school bus for fish.

Name It

LOOK at each picture. READ the words next to the picture. CIRCLE the word that matches the picture.

 cat   car   can

 bus   but   was

 coat   bit   boat

 trick   tuck   truck

 rain   train   tan

 plane   plan   plate

Order Up!

MATCH each picture with a sentence. WRITE the number of the picture next to the sentence it matches. Now READ the story in the correct order.

The truck went on the train.

But I went on the plane!

The car went on the truck.

The train went on the boat.

Hide and Speak

READ each word out loud. DRAW a line from each word to something in the picture that matches it.

car

bus

boat

truck

train

plane

Story Time

READ the words. Then READ the story. CIRCLE the words as you find them.

car   bus   boat   truck   train   plane

I put my train in a box.

I put in my plane too.

Then I put in a car and a bus.

Mom put the box on the truck.

"Wait!" I said.

I ran back into the house.

I almost forgot my boat!

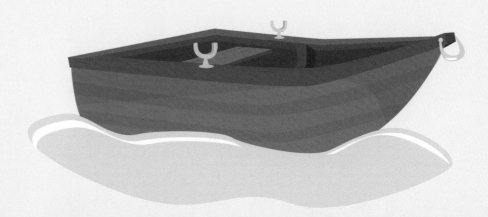

Jiffy Words

Say It

LOOK at the words. READ each word out loud. Then READ each word out loud again in a spooky voice.

Space Trace

Space Ace found words in the stars! TRACE the words so he can read them.

saw

that

this

said

who

what

Word Blocks

SAY the words. FILL IN each word block with a word of the same shape.

saw   that   said   who   what

1.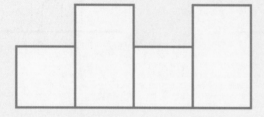

2.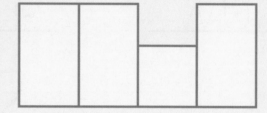

3.

4.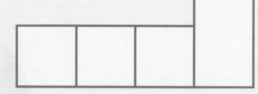

5.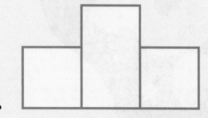

Word Hunt

READ the words. CIRCLE the words in the grid. WRITE each word after you circle it. Words go across and down.

this	that	said	who	what

w	w	h	o	t
t	h	i	s	h
s	a	i	d	m
a	t	h	a	t

Jiffy Words

Blank Out

READ each word. LOOK at each picture. WRITE the word to complete each sentence.

HINT: Each word is used only once.

saw	what	this	said	who

I know _____ is at the door!
1

I like _____ ball.
2

She _____ a big bug.
3

"Mine!" _____ the baby.
4

Do you know _____ time it is?
5

Spot the Dots

READ each word in the box. LOOK for only those words in the picture. DRAW a line to connect the words in ABC order, as they appear in the box. FIND the mystery picture!

HINT: "Who" is a word said by this bird.

| said | saw | that | this | what | who |

Match It

READ each word. DRAW a line from each word to the correct picture.

egg

leg

train

head

car

Poetry Guy

Help Poetry Guy write his poems. READ the words. FILL IN words that rhyme.

who	that	boat	head

My friend Ned
_____
has five hats on his _____.
1

I wonder _____
2

put an egg in my shoe.

What is _____?
3

Oh! Just a cat!

I have a _____,
4

but it does not float.

Start Your Crayons!

READ the words. COLOR only the dinosaurs that are wearing the words from the box.

what   hand   was   has   bus   head   saw

Try to Remember

CUT OUT the cards. READ the rules. PLAY the game!

Rules: Two players

1. MIX UP the cards.
2. PLACE the cards face down on a table.
3. TAKE TURNS turning over two cards at a time.
4. KEEP the cards when you match two words.

How many matches can you collect?

and	and	has	has
was	was	hand	hand
said	said	saw	saw
this	this	that	that

Answers

Page 128

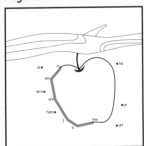

Page 129
1. is
2. are
3. I
4. a
5. am
6. the

Page 130
1. a
2. is
3. are
4. am

Page 131

Page 132
1. run
2. can
3. come
4. find
5. see

Page 133
1. run
2. see
3. come
4. can

Page 134

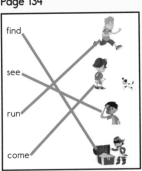

Page 135

I come home from school.
I run into the house.
I see a box!
I find my name on it.
Yay!
I can open the box!

Page 136

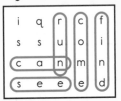

Page 137

Page 139

Page 140
1. big
2. little
3. pretty
4. long

Page 141
Have someone check
your answers.

Page 142

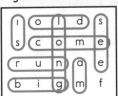

Page 143
1. pretty
2. I
3. little
4. the
5. find
6. can

Page 144

Page 145

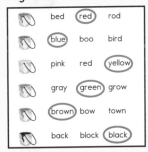

Page 146

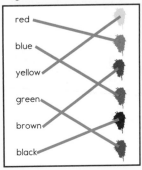

Page 147
1. blue
2. red
3. black
4. yellow
5. green
6. brown

Page 148

Page 149
Have someone check
your answers.

Page 150

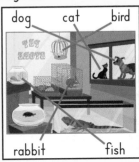

Page 151

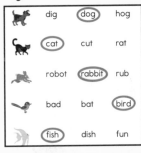

Page 152

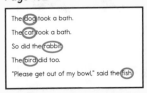

Page 153

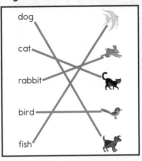

Page 154
Have someone check
your answers.

Answers

Page 155

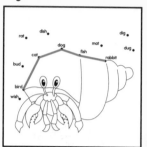

Page 158

1. not   2. at
3. will   4. to
5. say   6. an

Page 159

1. not   2. to
3. will   4. an

Page 160

Page 161

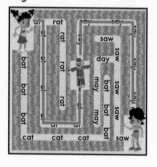

Page 163

1. she   2. he
3. me   4. you
5. it

Page 164

Page 165

Page 166

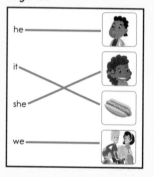

Page 167

Page 168

1. green   2. are
3. you   4. fish
5. a

Page 171

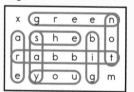

Page 172

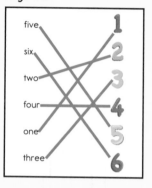

Page 173

Page 174

1. two   2. six
3. one   4. four
5. five   6. three

Page 175

Page 176

Page 177

Page 178

1. doll   2. ball
3. girl   4. boy
5. toy

Page 179

Page 181

1. play   2. get
3. ride   4. go
5. work

Page 182

1. play   2. get
3. go   4. work
5. ride

Page 183

1. go   2. play
3. get   4. ride

Page 184

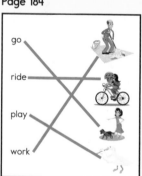

Answers

Page 185

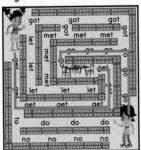

Page 186

4. Now we can play!
3. Get the brown rabbit.
1. Get the red toy.
2. Get the big ball.

Page 187

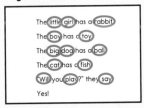

The little girl has a rabbit.
The boy has a toy.
The big dog has a ball.
The cat has a fish.
"Will you play?" they say.
Yes!

Page 188

Page 189

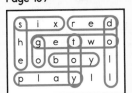

Page 191

1. make
2. give
3. look
4. like
5. want

Page 192

Page 193

1. want
2. give
3. like
4. make
5. look

Page 194

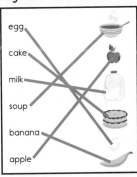

Page 195

Page 196

2. He put in milk.
4. Look! A cake!
1. I put in an egg.
3. She put in a banana.

Page 197

Have someone check
your answers.

Page 198

Page 199

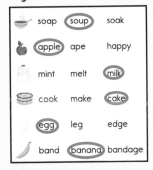

Page 201

1. out
2. up
3. down
4. on
5. under

Page 202

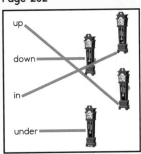

Page 203

1. down
2. under
3. in
4. on
5. up

Page 204

Page 205

2. The turtle went in the water.
4. The turtle stuck out his head to say "Good-bye!"
3. The turtle went under the water.
1. The bird sat on the turtle.

Page 206

Page 209

1. make
2. look
3. under
4. like

Page 212

1. for
2. yes
3. but
4. no
5. and

Page 213

Page 215

1. do
2. have
3. has
4. my
5. be

Answers

Page 216

I have four legs.

She has a doll.

I do not have fur.

Yes, my bird is green.

Page 217
1. do
2. my
3. be
4. was

Page 218

Page 219

Page 220

feet   leg   eyes

hand   head

Page 221

foot	(feet)	fee
(leg)	log	beg
I	(eyes)	yes
band	had	(hand)
(head)	had	hid

Page 222
4. But only one hand!
1. I see a head.
3. I see lots of feet.
2. I see eyes.

Page 223
1. eyes
2. head
3. leg
4. feet
5. hand

Page 224

The dog licked my (hand)
He sat by my (feet)
Then he put his (head) on my leg.
I looked at his big brown (eyes)
I will ask Dad if we can keep him!

Page 225

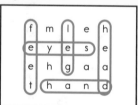

f	m	l	e	h
e	y	e	s	e
e	h	h	g	a
t	h	a	n	d

Page 226

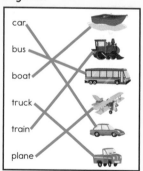

car
bus
boat
truck
train
plane

Page 227
Have someone check
your answers.

Page 228

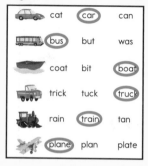

cat	(car)	can
(bus)	but	was
coat	bit	(boat)
trick	tuck	(truck)
rain	(train)	tan
(plane)	plan	plate

Page 229
2. The truck went on the train.
4. But I went on the plane!
1. The car went on the truck.
3. The train went on the boat.

Page 230

car   bus   boat

truck   train   plane

Page 231

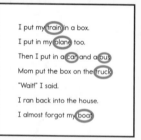

I put my (train) in a box.
I put in my (plane) too.
Then I put in a (car) and a (bus)
Mom put the box on the (truck)
"Wait!" I said.
I ran back into the house.
I almost forgot my (boat)

Page 234
1. what
2. that
3. saw
4. said
5. who

Page 235

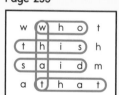

w	(w	h	o)	t
(t	h	i	s)	h
(s	a	i	d)	m
a	(t	h	a	t)

Page 236
1. who
2. this
3. saw
4. said
5. what

Page 237

Page 238

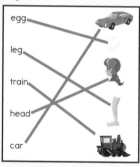

egg
leg
train
head
car

Page 239
1. head
2. who
3. that
4. boat

Page 240

246

Sylvan for Every Student!

SINGLE-SUBJECT WORKBOOKS

☑ Focus on individual skills and subjects

☑ Fun activities and grade-appropriate exercises

3-IN-1 SUPER WORKBOOKS

☑ Three Sylvan single-subject workbooks in one package for just $18.99!

☑ Perfect practice for the student who needs to focus on a range of topics

FUN ON THE RUN ACTIVITY BOOKS

☑ Just $3.99/$4.75 Can.

☑ Colorful games and activities for on-the-go learning

FLASHCARD SETS

☑ Spelling and vocabulary for Pre-K–5th grade

☑ Math for Pre-K–5th grade

PAGE PER DAY WORKBOOKS

☑ Perforated pages—perfect for your child to do just one workbook page each day

☑ Extra practice the easy way!

KICK START PACKAGES

☑ Includes books, flashcards, access to online activities, and more

☑ Everything your child needs in one comprehensive package

Try FREE pages today at SylvanPagePerDay.com

Sylvan Learning